GO
and
make
disciples!

Jer. 29:11,
"For il know the plans il have
for you," declares the Lord, "plans to
prosper you, and not to harm you,
plans to give you hope and a future."

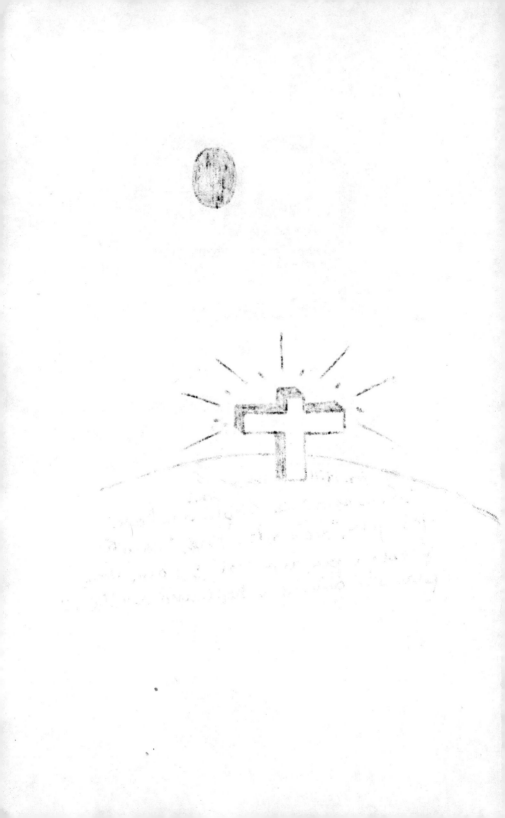

GO
and
make
disciples!

An Introduction to Christian Missions

ROGER S. GREENWAY

P&R PUBLISHING

P.O BOX 817 • PHILLIPSBURG • NEW JERSEY 08865-0817

Typesetting by Michelle Feaster

Printed in the United States of America

Library of Congress Cataloging-in-Publication Data

Greenway, Roger S.
    Go and make disciples! : an introduction to Christian missions/
    Roger S. Greenway.
        p. cm.
    Includes bibliographical references and indexes.
    ISBN 0-87552-218-1 (pbk.)
    1. Missions—Theory. I. Title.
    BV2063.G74 1999
    266—dc21   99–039292

✐❧ Contents

𝒞𝓋 Preface

Go and Make Disciples! is for readers who want a book about missions written in plain language. This book will help readers understand missions and challenge them to apply Christ's missionary command to themselves and their churches. It is easy to read and easy to translate into other languages. Readers whose second or third language is English should find the words simple and clear.

This book is based on six important truths.

(1) Jesus Christ commanded his disciples to take the gospel to the whole world. He intended missions to be the continual responsibility of the whole church until Christ himself returns.

(2) The Holy Spirit raises up missionaries from all nations, races, and societies. Missionaries are people who proclaim the gospel in places where spiritual darkness is the greatest. There are at this moment more missionaries from non-Western countries than from Western countries. The twenty-first century will be the greatest century of missions, and its greatest strength will be in the non-Western part of the world.

(3) The Bible is our authority in missions. The Bible reveals the message of the gospel, the right motives for missions, and the goals and methods that please God. There is an urgent need to train leaders for mission work that is inspired and directed by biblical teaching.

(4) The study of missions is important for pastors, teachers, leaders of local churches, and students preparing for

Christian ministry. Christians need to be informed about missions and challenged personally by the "Great Commission" that Christ gave the church.

(5) Christians need to share with one another what the Bible teaches and what they have learned by experience about the important subject of missions. This means that Christians from East and West, North and South must communicate with one another about missions.

(6) Passion for God and a burning desire that God alone be worshipped everywhere is the fuel that keeps the fire of missions burning. The Spirit of God will continue to inspire men and women to missions until the prophecy of Habakkuk 2:14 is fulfilled: "For the earth will be filled with the knowledge of the glory of the LORD, as the waters cover the sea." Missions will continue until that day dawns!

No book has all the answers to the question of how to evangelize the world in the most effective way. Each country and each culture are different. Circumstances change from one time and place to another. The twenty-first century will be different from all earlier periods of history. New ways to communicate the gospel continue to be discovered.

Jesus said, "Go and make disciples." The word that is translated "Go" in the original Greek language is in a form that expresses great urgency. Jesus meant to say, "Get going! Do not delay! Multiply until people of all nations, races, tribes, and languages know and follow me!"

I offer this book to servants of Christ in every part of the world who sincerely desire to honor Christ, build his church, and extend his kingdom by obeying his Great Commission. Remember his words, and do as he leads you.

A Word of Gratitude

I am grateful above all to the triune God, the Author of missions. I would also like to thank

- Harold Kallemeyn for opening my eyes to the need for a textbook on missions for non-Western students;
- Calvin Theological Seminary for giving me time to write this book, and the Faculty Heritage Fund for financial assistance;
- Marcia and Mark Van Drunen for their editing and technical assistance;
- David Luikaart for his help in worldwide distribution;
- all the writers, students, and co-workers who gave me ideas and shared their experiences in the work of missions;
- the teachers and translators in different countries who will make this book their tool to inspire followers of Christ to hear, understand, and obey his Great Commission.

 PART 1

The World to Which Christ Sends Us

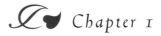 Chapter 1

Worldwide Challenges

These are exciting times in which to follow Christ and obey his command, "Go and make disciples" (Matthew 28:19). The missionary challenges throughout the world have never been greater than they are now. We need to know about these challenges and consider what they mean for the kingdom of Christ and its growth. Therefore, in this opening chapter I will place before you ten important challenges that have great importance for Christian missions.

POPULATION GROWTH

The population of the world was probably not more than 300 million when Jesus spoke the Great Commission. Now the world population is around six billion—and growing. Most of the population growth is in Asia, Latin America, Africa, and countries whose principal religion is not Christianity. More than half the world worships some other god than the God revealed in the Bible and in Jesus Christ.

What does this mean for Christian missions? Clearly, it means that the harvest field is larger than ever before. More people need to be reached with the gospel. More workers need to respond to the Lord's call, prepare themselves, and begin gathering the harvest. Churches everywhere must become involved in missions by praying for, supporting, and sending missionaries.

This is not a time to reduce missionary efforts, but to increase them by enlisting churches everywhere in the work of making disciples of Christ.

POPULATION MOVEMENTS

People are moving from one place to another as never before, creating new challenges and opportunities to reach others with the gospel.

The first kind of population movement is migration to the cities. We have seen the greatest migration in human history in the past twenty years, as over a billion people left their traditional homes on farms and in small villages and moved to cities. This migration to the cities means that masses of people now live close together and can be reached more easily through evangelism. Studies show that many people are more open to listening to the gospel when in a new environment.

Second, there are more people migrating from one country to another than we have ever seen before. People from the Southern hemisphere are moving north, and people from the East are moving west. People from the Middle East are everywhere. In most cases, immigrants settle in urban areas. This turns cities into international communities with people of many different races, cultures, religions, and languages.

Third, there are more refugees throughout the world than ever before. Refugees are the victims of war, political struggle, natural disasters, or drought. They are forced to leave their traditional places of living and to search for new homes. When they are living as refugees, they often show interest in the Christian faith for the first time.

International students represent a fourth type of population movement. Tens of thousands of students leave home every year and go to some distant place in order to gain more education. It may be the first time for some of them that they come into contact with the church and the gospel. International students are a great missionary challenge, and we as the church need to do more to draw them to Christ.

DOORS THAT SUDDENLY OPEN

One thing we have learned in missions is that doors that were tightly closed for many years may suddenly open. God gives us a new opportunity to spread his Word when this happens, and we must be ready to respond. At the sight of every open door, we hear Jesus say again, "Go and make disciples!"

In some countries it was impossible to distribute Bibles or preach the gospel ten or twenty years ago. Today such activities are done freely. This gives us confidence when we think of places that remain closed. There is no door too difficult for God to open. He works according to his schedule and in his own way.

CULTURAL BARRIERS

Some of the greatest challenges we face in missions are due to cultural barriers: differences in language, custom, religion, values, and attitudes. Cultural barriers separate people and make it difficult for the message of Christ to move from one group to another.

For this reason, missionary training includes the study of cultures and how to communicate the gospel from one culture to another. It is a mistake to think that cultural barriers will disappear soon. Some cultural barriers, on the contrary, appear to be increasing.

The church grows everywhere on earth through missions, and people from different cultures come together in one great

Body. This is what Jesus commanded us to do when he said, "Go and make disciples *of all nations.*"

"All nations" is *panta ta ethne* in the ancient Greek language of the New Testament, and it means *all peoples, tribes,* and *races.* It is not surprising, therefore, that the Body of Christ is the largest multicultural community on earth, and it continues to grow.

THE STRENGTH OF NON-CHRISTIAN RELIGIONS

Large numbers of people today embrace the great non-Christian religions—Islam, Hinduism, and Buddhism. Wherever the majority of the population follows one of these religions, the spread of the gospel is opposed. Christian missionaries have difficulty getting visas to enter these countries. Local Christians may be persecuted in a variety of ways. Religious workers are the targets of attacks, and some may be killed.

In addition to places where non-Christian religions have traditionally been strong, they are growing in Western countries. Part of the growth is due to the migration of Muslims, Hindus, and Buddhists to the West. Their high birth rate also contributes to their growing numbers.

There are now more Muslims than evangelical Christians in France. There are now large mosques in countries where traditionally there were almost no Muslims. Courses in Buddhism and Hinduism are popular at universities in North America. Spiritism and superstitions that some people thought had disappeared are attracting new followers.

All this means that "mission fields" are everywhere, in the East and the West, the North and the South. Christians everywhere must be ready to defend and explain the gospel. Churches everywhere must become *missionary* communities. Leaders must be able to explain the message of Christ to many kinds of people.

THE GROWTH OF MISSIONS BASED IN ASIA, AFRICA, AND LATIN AMERICA

The number of missionaries coming from Asia, Africa, and Latin America has risen greatly in recent years. Christian missions no longer come mainly from the West. The total number of missionaries from non-Western countries now exceeds the number coming from Europe and America.

Many non-Western missionaries are going to places where it is difficult to live and where resistance to the gospel is strong. They are finding ways to enter countries where Western missionaries cannot go. They are showing that Christianity is neither a "religion of white men" nor a religion that only Western people want. When someone from the Philippines or Korea or Brazil stands up and preaches the message of Christ, it is a powerful witness to the fact that Jesus is indeed the "Savior of the world" (John 4:42).

Churches in all parts of the world are awakening to their responsibility to participate in world missions. It can be said as never before that the *whole church* is bringing the *whole gospel* to the *whole world*. This was what Jesus wanted when he commanded the men who became the first leaders of the church to "go and make disciples."

WESTERN COUNTRIES ARE NOW MISSION FIELDS

There are many Christian institutions and mission organizations located in the West. It is a sad fact, however, that in most of Europe, Canada, and the United States, Christianity has lost much of the moral and religious strength it had in the past.

Most missionaries came from Western countries during the past two centuries, but Western countries have become mission fields. They need to be evangelized again. Meanwhile, the centers of missionary power are moving to other parts of the world.

THE NEW FACE OF THE CHURCH AND NEW CENTERS OF MISSIONS

The face of the church has changed because the majority of Christians now live in Asia, Africa, and Latin America. It is predicted that by the year 2025, only 25 percent of Christians will live in Western countries. The centers of Christian education as well as missions increasingly are moving from the West to the South and the East. Christian leaders of the twenty-first century will be mainly from these new centers.

Asia already has the majority of the world's people. Asia also has the largest numbers of non-Christians. What does this mean for missions? Asian Christians must join with their brothers and sisters from other parts of the world to complete the task of missions.

Something more must be said. Some parts of the world are becoming more hostile to Christianity. Christian workers must be prepared for difficulties. Muslims are already strong and organized opponents. Hindus are becoming more hostile to Christian work. Therefore Christians, and especially missionaries and church leaders, must prepare for the growing challenges and even for persecution.

POVERTY IS INCREASING

The sad fact is that the number of poor people is increasing. The challenge to missions is to show Christian compassion in ways that will help the poor escape from poverty, while at the same time telling them about Jesus Christ.

Two facts impress us when we examine this challenge.

1. *Generally speaking, the poor and the lost (spiritually) are the same people.*

A look at a world map shows that those countries that are furthest from Christ and the gospel are also the poorest countries. Likewise, they are countries in which there is a great deal of oppression and injustice. Therefore, we see a connection between spiritual bondage and physical suffering and injustice.

2. *The poor are the largest single group among all the people in the world that are outside the Christian faith.*

Some of them live in villages and some of them in large cities. Wherever they are, the poor and the lost call to us to bring them the gospel and Christian mercy. We must not ignore their cry.

CHILDREN AND YOUNG PEOPLE MAKE UP HALF OF THE POPULATION OF THE WORLD

There have never been so many children and young people before in all of human history. This represents a great challenge to Christian missions. Young people are the ones who make most of the decisions to follow Christ. Bringing the Word of God to young people requires special literature, teachers who are trained to work with youth, and programs designed for children and youth. More Christian workers are needed who will direct most of their efforts to reaching youth for Christ.

These are some of the major challenges to Christian missions around the world. It is clear that multitudes of people, some of them nearby and others far away, need to hear about Jesus, learn his Word, and feel the touch of his love.

Is a vision for missions taking shape in your mind? My vision, which I share with you, is that *nobody on earth will be allowed to die without hearing the gospel and feeling the mercy of God in a personal way.*

REVIEW QUESTIONS

1. List the challenges presented in this chapter.

2. Choose three that seem especially important to you and explain your choice.

3. Why is the church the largest multicultural community in the world?

DISCUSSION QUESTIONS

1. What did Jesus say that makes the needs of people everywhere in the world important to Christians?

2. What additional challenges can you suggest besides these ten?

3. Suggest some things that schools and churches can do in response to these challenges.

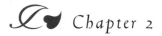 Chapter 2

Missionaries:
Co-workers with God

Mission(s) means *sending* and proceeds from the plan and purpose of God. The Baptist missiologist Francis M. DuBose says in his book *God Who Sends* that the biblical picture of the one true God is the picture of a great and continual "Sender." God sends to the earth rain and sunshine, storms and judgments in his providence. God sends his Word, his Son, his Spirit, and his servants in all times and places with his salvation.

> The language of sending describes the whole range of God's concern and activity in the world. He sent Samuel to deliver his people (1 Samuel 12:11) and to anoint Saul and David as kings (16:1). He sent the prophet Nathan to condemn King David for his sin (2 Samuel 12:1). He sent the prophets: Isaiah (6:8); Jeremiah (1:7); Elijah (2 Kings 2); Haggai (1:12); Zechariah (2:8). He repeatedly sent his prophets on missions to his people (Jeremiah 7:25; 25:4; 26:5; 29:19; 35:15). He sent John the Baptist as the forerunner of Jesus (John 1:6–8). He sent his angels (messengers) to testify to the churches (Revelation 22:16). He sent his Holy Spirit into the world (John 14:26; 1 Peter 1:12). (*God Who Sends*, 60)

JESUS, THE "SENT ONE" AND THE "SENDER"

Jesus brought together his own mission from the Father with the mission that he gave the disciples, when he said, "As the Father has sent me, I am sending you" (John 20:21). It is important to observe the order of the "sendings" in this passage. First, the Son of God was sent by the Father, and that makes Jesus the primary, divine Missionary. Jesus, in turn, sent his disciples, which made them missionaries of the gospel. We learn in other parts of the gospel of John that the Holy Spirit was sent by God to bear witness to Christ and convict the world of sin, righteousness, and judgment (John 14:25–6; 15:26–7; 16:7–8).

This is very significant for our understanding of missions. *Christ calls his followers, ALL of them, to be co-missioners and co-workers with him.* God calls us to participate with him in the work of evangelizing the world. Hearing this, every follower of Christ should respond from the heart like the Virgin Mary when she heard the announcement of the angel: "I am the Lord's servant. Let God's will for me be done" (Luke 1:38, my translation).

This is the glory of the missionary calling. We are followers of Christ and co-missioners with him. As he was sent and commissioned to bear witness to the truth, so we are sent and commissioned. In the power of the Holy Spirit we become co-participants in the plan and purpose of God to reconcile the world to himself. Missions is not only work *for* God, but work *with* God. The work is to be done in a way that resembles the sacrificial obedience of Jesus Christ.

KEY ELEMENTS IN CO-MISSIONING WITH GOD

In 1891 Arthur T. Pierson delivered a series of lectures on missions at the Reformed Seminar in New Brunswick Seminary, New Jersey. The nineteenth century, often called the "Great Century of Missions," was drawing to a close. Interest in

missions was great in England, Europe, and America. Night after night the auditorium was filled, with both students and
Christians from the wider community. Pierson spoke of missions as follows:

> In the New Testament . . . work for souls is set forth as
> a co-operation with the triune God in three various as-
> pects, as *co-labor, co-suffering,* and *co-witnessing.* But that
> which is far more remarkable and impressive . . . is that
> the Father, the Son, and the Holy Spirit are individu-
> ally, successively, and separately presented as personally
> sharing with the believer the dignity of this exalted
> service. (*The Divine Enterprise of Missions,* 104)

Missionaries are men and women who are given the honor
of being co-missioners with the triune God in proclaiming the
gospel to lost people. Their task has three elements: co-working,
co-suffering, and co-witnessing with God and fellow believers.
Look at these verses from the Word of God:

Co-working

> For we are God's fellow workers; you are . . . God's
> building. (1 Corinthians 3:9)

> As God's fellow workers we urge you not to receive
> God's grace in vain. (2 Corinthians 6:1)

Co-suffering

> Now I rejoice in what was suffered for you, and I fill up
> in my flesh what is still lacking in regard to Christ's af-
> flictions, for the sake of his body, which is the church.
> I have become its servant by the commission God gave
> me to present to you the word of God in its fullness.
> (Colossians 1:24–25)

Co-witnessing

> When the Counselor comes, whom I will send to you
> from the Father, the Spirit of truth who goes out from
> the Father, he will testify about me. And you also must
> testify, for you have been with me from the beginning.
> (John 15:26–27)

Missions is a divine enterprise, and it embraces the plan of
God for every one of his children. All believers have roles to
play in missions. God has appointed a time and a place for
everyone, and our highest duty in life is to find God's will for
us within his plan and carry it out.

We are called to build living temples to God the Father
who alone is worshipped. We call sinners to be reconciled to
God through the Son who suffered for our sins. We bear witness with the Spirit to the truth about God and redemption
through Jesus Christ as revealed in the Bible.

What a picture this is! The imperfect efforts of believers
are incorporated into the perfect work of God in finding the
lost and building the church. God so designed his saving plan
for the world that the plan cannot be completed without the
participation of believers in the work of missions.

CO-WORKING WITH GOD

The gospel needs a voice; God planned it that way. The good
news about Jesus Christ cannot announce itself. It must have a
human announcer. John the Baptist said, "I am the voice"
(John 1:23). Not merely a sound or noise, but a clear, intelli-
gent human voice was required to point people to Jesus. This
has been true in every generation. God uses messengers. As
Paul said, "We are therefore Christ's ambassadors, as though
God were making his appeal through us" (2 Corinthians 5:20).

The word "ambassadors" conveys a number of important

truths. Ambassadors are official representatives sent from one government to another. By virtue of their appointment, ambassadors have the authority of the state that commissioned them. Ambassadors do not speak for themselves but for the government they represent, and behind them stands the power and authority of their government.

The same is true of the ambassadors of Christ who speak the truth of God and carry out his instructions. God speaks in and through them when they speak faithfully the Word of God. The power and authority of God stand behind them. People who receive them and believe their message receive Christ and his Father, and all he promises. Those who refuse to believe their message reject Christ and his Word. As Jesus said, "Whoever accepts anyone I send accepts me; and whoever accepts me accepts the one who sent me" (John 13:20).

CO-SUFFERING WITH CHRIST

What suffering must messengers of the gospel expect? Jesus told his disciples to expect suffering and opposition. Some of them would lose their lives for his sake and the gospel (Matthew 10:38–39). Following him would not be easy.

Persecution and the proclamation of the gospel often go together because persecution is one way people resist the gospel. The purpose of persecution is to damage the church and prevent the gospel from spreading. Persecution often takes away the leaders of the church.

The apostle Paul wrote that he rejoiced in his sufferings, and he called his sufferings "Christ's afflictions, for the sake of his body, which is the church" (Colossians 1:24). Paul also spoke of the spiritual benefits of suffering (Romans 5:3–5). He regarded a godly life that was free of suffering to be a rare exception (2 Timothy 3:12).

Some Christians live in "exceptional" countries that enjoy religious freedom. They know little about persecution and suffering with Christ. Other Christians know a great deal about it because they live in places where Christians pay a high price for their faith and witness.

Persecution aimed at Christians is increasing in many parts of the world. Pastors, evangelists, and other Christian leaders are usually the primary targets of persecution. Christians may be punished, even killed, simply for worshipping God. They may be charged with crimes they never committed. Some minor offense may be treated as a major crime. Christian young people may not be admitted to universities, and better jobs may be closed to them. In extreme cases, Christian children are taken from their parents, and young girls are forced to marry men of another religion.

Missionaries and evangelists carry the gospel into places where Satan and idolatry have controlled the hearts of many people for centuries, so they must expect opposition. Christ may call them to witness for him unto suffering and death. They should never invite persecution by needlessly offending others or by provoking social disorder. If persecution comes, however, they should accept it in faith. By the grace of God, it can be a blessing.

CO-WITNESSING WITH THE HOLY SPIRIT

In John 14–16, Jesus promised that the Holy Spirit would come and be his continuing witness. The Spirit would empower the disciples to know and understand the truth and declare it to the world. The special office of the Spirit is to bear witness to Christ through the lives and from the lips of believers.

Early disciples expressed co-witnessing with the Spirit as they stood up against persecution before the leaders of the Jews. They testified, "We are witnesses of these things [about Jesus and the resurrection], and so is the Holy Spirit, whom God has given to those who obey him" (Acts 5:32).

This co-witnessing of human witnesses with the divine witness of the Holy Spirit is of highest importance. Believers proclaim by words and actions the facts and meaning of the gospel. The Spirit empowers their witness and does with it what they themselves cannot do. The Spirit witnesses *internally* while the people of God witness *externally*. Their witness is important, but it can never go beyond physical eyes and ears. Only the witness of the Spirit can speak with a voice that reaches the soul and changes the heart.

The same pattern has continued throughout the history of Christian missions, since the time of the early apostles. The Spirit has used, empowered, and worked through the witness of Christ's servants to communicate the gospel to lost people. It is the only way he works, so far as we know. The Spirit employs human co-witnesses in the divine activity of applying the saving work of Christ to human hearts and lives.

REVIEW QUESTIONS

1. What does Francis DuBose mean when he speaks of God as "the God who sends"?

2. What are the three key elements in co-missioning with God? Quote the texts that teach these key elements.

3. Why are suffering and persecution inevitable when the gospel is spreading?

4. Explain why "co-witnessing" is so important and necessary.

DISCUSSION QUESTIONS

1. Tell the group your personal story of coming to know Jesus and how God used human co-witnesses to lead you to him.

2. In a Muslim or Hindu community, what actions might provoke persecution unnecessarily?

3. What things are Christians who live in hostile communities obliged to do regardless of the consequences?

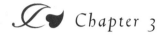 *Chapter 3*

Motives for Missions

Why do missions? Why do Christians tell others about their faith and try to persuade them to follow Jesus? Why do churches send missionaries and support them with their gifts? What motivates the many activities that bear the name "Christian missions," and what do they seek to accomplish?

Non-Christians often describe missions in terms of religious and cultural imperialism. They think that missionaries are proud people who believe their religion and culture are better than anyone else's. Many non-Christians doubt that missions is good for their country and people.

Even Christians sometimes question the need for missions. Some Christians lack instruction from the Word of God on the subject of missions. Some have heard things that raise doubts about the motives and goals of missionaries. In some countries there has been hostility toward Christian missions for a long time, but there is also a growing opposition in places where people were tolerant of mission activity in the past. This leads some to ask, Should Christians reduce their missionary efforts in order to avoid problems, or is telling a Christian not to share his faith like telling a fish not to swim? These are important questions, and Christians should be able to answer them.

Wrong Motives for Missions

First of all, we must admit that there have always been people who entered the work of the Lord for the wrong reasons. Even missionaries with right motives may make mistakes, and sometimes it is difficult to work with them. Missions does not lose its validity, however, just because missionaries make mistakes and some have unworthy motives.

We should remember the days of the apostles. John Mark abandoned Paul and Barnabas on their first missionary journey (Acts 13:13). The disagreement over whether to give John Mark a second chance so divided Paul and Barnabas that they went their separate ways (Acts 15:37–40). There was also the sad story of Demas, who deserted Paul at a critical time "because he loved this world" (2 Timothy 4:10). These experiences disappointed the apostles but did not change their convictions regarding the importance of missions.

Some wrong motives for becoming a missionary are

- a desire to be admired and praised by others;
- a search for "self-fulfillment," without regard for self-emptying (Philippians 2:5–7);
- the pursuit of adventure and excitement;
- ambition to expand the glory and influence of a particular church, denomination, or country;
- escape from unpleasant situations at home;
- hope for professional advancement after a short period of mission service;
- guilt, and a desire for peace with God through missionary service.

There may be elements of wrong motives hidden in the minds of even the most sincere missionaries. We should be aware that wrong motives might be present, and repent from them when they are discovered. We must ask God to replace them with right motives so that our service may be pure and acceptable to him.

RIGHT MOTIVES FOR MISSIONS

Right motives for missions are taught in the Word of God and made alive in the hearts of believers by the Holy Spirit. Such motives do not change over the years, and they apply to missionaries and their supporters from every country in the world. Right motives are the following:

1. *The desire that God be worshipped and his glory known among all the peoples of the earth.*

The glory of God means everything revealed about God: his name, his holiness, his mighty power, his saving love in Jesus Christ; his mercy, grace, and righteousness. The chief end of all human existence, says the first question and answer of the Westminster Shorter Catechism, is to bring glory to God and enjoy him forever.

More than three billion people in the world, however, do not worship the one true God. They also do not enjoy fellowship with him. They worship other gods instead, or no god at all. The purpose of their lives is not to praise God but to satisfy themselves.

The thought that so many people do not worship God stirs missionaries and their supporters to action. They cannot rest until idolatry is replaced by true worship. They sense a divine compulsion to preach the gospel (1 Corinthians 9:16). They want the Word of God proclaimed and his name honored by people everywhere whatever the cost.

2. *The desire to obey God out of love and gratitude by carrying out Christ's commission to "go and make disciples of all nations" (Matthew 28:19).*

This motive for missions naturally follows the first. "If you love me," said Jesus, "you will obey what I command" (John 14:15). Genuine love for God produces obedience to his Word, and nothing is clearer than Christ's command to go and make disciples of all nations and peoples.

Christian obedience takes many forms, and the people of God are anointed by the Holy Spirit to serve God in a variety of ministries (1 Corinthians 12:4–5). Does not the kingdom of God on earth consist of the multitude of believers in Christ who, out of gratitude to God, seek to bring glory to God by obeying his commands in the power of the Holy Spirit?

Missionaries are people within this multitude of God's servants who believe that God calls them to a particular form of obedience. They believe God calls them to proclaim the gospel to unsaved people. Missionaries often talk about this personal "call" to missions because it plays a powerful, motivating role in their ministries. This sense of God's personal call to mission work is especially important in times of difficulty.

However, the call to missions is not entirely an individual matter. Christ assigns to his church the task of bringing the gospel to the world (Ephesians 3:10). This implies that a personal call to missions needs to be recognized and supported by a congregation of believers. This is also the biblical pattern (Acts 13:2–3; 14:26). By sending and supporting missionaries, the entire church participates in Christ's missionary command.

3. *A burning desire to use every legitimate means to save the lost and win unbelievers to faith in Christ.*

Paul describes his missionary motivation this way:

> Though I am free and belong to no man, I make myself a slave to everyone, to *win* as many as possible. To the Jews I became like a Jew, to *win* the Jews. To those under the law I became like one under the law . . . so as to *win* those under the law. To those not having the law I became like one not having the law . . . so as to *win* those not having the law. To the weak I became weak, to *win* the weak. I have become all things to all

men so that by all possible means I might *save* some. (1
Corinthians 9:19–22)

These are clearly the words of a missionary who was deeply
motivated by a passion to see lost people reconciled to God
and made heirs of eternal life by faith in Christ. Paul was not
so foolish as to think that he could save people by his own
strength. He knew that saving faith is a sovereign gift of God
(Ephesians 2:8). Paul also knew that missionaries were necessary in the carrying out of God's purpose. Under the inspiration of the Holy Spirit, Paul said,

> All this is from God, who reconciled us to himself
> through Christ and gave us the ministry of reconciliation:
> that God was reconciling the world to himself in Christ,
> not counting men's sins against them. And he has com-
> mitted to us the message of reconciliation. We are there-
> fore Christ's ambassadors, as though God were making
> his appeal through us. We implore you on Christ's be-
> half: Be reconciled to God. (2 Corinthians 5:18–20)

The missionary's passion for the glory of God is accompanied by a passion for people who through ignorance and un-
belief are dying in sin. Was not this Jesus' passion in Luke 15
when he told the parables of the lost sheep, the lost coin, and
the lost son? This passion moves missionaries to actions that are
designed to bring glory to God through the salvation of sinners.

4. *Concern that churches grow and multiply, and that the
   kingdom of Christ be extended by words and deeds that
   proclaim the compassion and righteousness of Christ to
   a world of suffering and injustice.*

Christ came preaching the kingdom of God, and he established the church as its bright light and example. As a bright
light, the church draws people to Christ, who saves, comforts,
and heals. The church models to the world what life in the king-

dom is about. Through the church, the world gets a look at the fellowship of redeemed and reconciled people, who practice love, faithfulness, truth, and righteousness, though imperfectly. The church also works to promote these same virtues in society.

Because they are aware of the biblical emphasis on churches, missionaries plant and nourish congregations of believers wherever they can. They proclaim the gospel with words and demonstrate the gospel with deeds of mercy. They point to Jesus Christ, the Savior, Healer, Leader, Deliverer, and Friend, the Head of the church (Colossians 1:18), by both their words and their deeds.

A Sense of Urgency

Missionaries seem to be restless people. They are always coming or going, studying maps, or planning to explore some new place. Missionaries always seem to be talking about evangelism, unreached people, and new strategies for spreading the gospel. They tell stories about people whose lives were changed and about the misery in which some people live.

Missionaries also seem to be restless about the church. They refuse to allow churches to be lazy. Missionaries are always challenging Christians to more prayer, wider outreach, more giving, and more workers. There is a sense of urgency with missionaries, as though precious time is slipping away.

I think this sense of urgency comes from their awareness of the needs of lost and suffering people, the greatness of the gospel, and the urging of the Holy Spirit, who will not rest until God's missionary purpose for the world is finished.

The Final Goal of Missions

We read in the book of Revelation about the vision John had of the great multitude that some day will be gathered before the throne of Jesus Christ. The multitude is made up of people bought by the blood of Christ from "every tribe and language and people and nation" (Revelation 5:9). They never cease worshipping and praising the Lord.

Reading that passage, everyone involved in missions exclaims, "That is my vision! That is the goal! When the work is finished, God will be worshipped by a great multitude of redeemed people, who are gathered from the whole human race. The enemies of Christ and the misery they cause will be gone, and life will be restored to the way it ought to be. Now, to that end, I dedicate my life, resources, and energy!"

"Why do missions?" With such a vision before us, how can we *not* do missions?

REVIEW QUESTIONS

1. Give some of the wrong reasons for missions.

2. Why can elements of wrong motives be found even in sincere missionaries?

3. What are the four right motives for missions?

4. Why do missionaries seem "restless"?

DISCUSSION QUESTIONS

1. Suggest ways in which the church serves as a "showcase" of the kingdom.

2. Explain what you think the author means by "lazy" churches and complacent Christians. Suggest some examples.

3. The next time you hear people talking negatively about missions, how will you respond?

 *PART* 2

The Biblical Foundation
of Missions

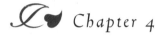 Chapter 4

The Old Testament Basis of Missions

"If you want to evangelize Hindus and Buddhists, you must begin with the Old Testament, starting with Genesis 1–3," advised my missionary colleague and mentor, Richard De Ridder. We were together on the island of Sri Lanka, known as Ceylon in those days. I was fresh out of school, and he was an experienced pastor and missionary. I took his advice, and it helped me a great deal. It will also help us understand the biblical foundations of Christian missions.

J. H. Bavinck, the Dutch missions scholar who spent many years as a missionary to Indonesia, observes,

> At first sight the Old Testament appears to offer little basis for the idea of missions. . . . Yet, if we investigate the Old Testament more thoroughly, it becomes clear that the future of the nations is a point of the greatest concern. . . . This indeed cannot be otherwise, for from the first page to the last the Bible has the whole world in view, and its divine plan of salvation is unfolded as pertaining to the whole world. (*An Introduction to the Science of Missions*, 11)

Bavinck points out that without Genesis 1.1 there would be no Matthew 28.19–20. The God who sent his Son, Jesus, to become the Savior of the world is the God who created the heavens and the earth and made all the peoples of the world of one blood. God not only creates the world, but he governs it and holds all his creatures responsible to him. He wants all nations to worship him alone. God's call to Abraham and his descendants, the people of Israel, to be separate from other nations was part of his plan to bring the blessing of salvation to all peoples (Genesis 12:3).

Bavinck sees indications in the Old Testament prophets that there will one day be a great turning of the Gentiles to Christ. They will be moved to come by God. This will provoke the Jews to jealousy and in the last days Jews will follow Gentiles to the Lord, and the Lord will be honored by Israel once again (Ezekiel 36:22–23). God, the Creator and Redeemer of both Gentiles and Jews, is behind this.

MISSIONS INVOLVES CONFLICT OVER WORLDVIEWS

The Old Testament shows us that the basic point of difference between the religion of the Bible and all other faiths is a matter of different *worldviews*. Worldviews are the beliefs that people hold regarding the most important questions of life.

In missions, Christians proclaim their distinctive Christian worldview—as found in the Bible—to people who hold non-Christian worldviews. By urging non-Christians to follow Christ, Christians challenge non-Christians to choose between the two worldviews. Below are a number of worldview questions:

- Does God exist? If so, what is the nature of God?
- How did the world begin, and for what purpose?
- What are human beings? Are we merely smart animals, or something more?
- What causes evil and suffering?

- Is there an invisible world of spirits, some of them good and others bad?
- Is there life after death?
- How can people be saved?

BLAUW AND HEDLUND ON OLD TESTAMENT FOUNDATIONS OF MISSIONS

Johannes Blauw and Roger E. Hedlund are two scholars who have written about Old Testament foundations of Christian missions. Blauw points out that God had his eye on all nations and peoples from the very beginning. The *universal* concern of God is clearest in the Old Testament in Isaiah 40–55 and the book of Jonah. Blauw says,

> There is real justification for speaking of a missionary calling *of Israel.* Israel is called, under the figure of the Servant, to bring justice to the nations, and to bring light to the nations. Certainly the command to missions can be formulated no more clearly than that. (*The Missionary Nature of the Church,* 32)

Roger E. Hedlund discusses the importance of Genesis for missions in his book *The Mission of the Church in the World.* Hedlund has a deep understanding of Asian worldviews because he lived and wrote in India. He saw clearly that the biblical worldview is very different from all other religious worldviews, and in this lies the importance of Christian missions.

THE WORLDVIEW OF THE BIBLE VERSUS OTHERS

1. *The God of the Bible and Gods of the Nations*

Genesis 1:1 sets forth the most basic of all truths in the Christian worldview: "In the beginning God created the heavens and the earth." This one verse teaches the following:

- *Theism:* Genesis begins by affirming that God exists and that he existed before the world began. God alone is eternal, and material things are temporal. The belief that there is no god is completely denied.
- *Biblical monotheism:* People worship many different gods and goddesses in our world, but the Bible reveals the person and nature of the one true God and Creator of all things.
- *Exclusivism:* The one God demands exclusive worship and obedience. No other gods and no other worship are permitted (Exodus 20:3–4). Moses said that the gods of the nations are not gods but demons and should not be worshipped in any form (Deuteronomy 32:16–18).

2. The Nature of God as Creator of the Universe

Genesis teaches that *polytheism,* the idea that there are many gods, is false. There are invisible spirits called angels and demons, which God created, but God alone is to be worshipped and served. This shows the great difference between the biblical worldview and the worldview of billions of people who worship gods of various kinds. It is obvious, therefore, that in missions we deal with conflicts between contradictory worldviews. The most basic aspect of the biblical worldview has to do with the nature of God.

Genesis denies *pantheism,* the idea that God is in everything and there is no real distinction between God and the material world. Genesis teaches that in creating the universe God brought into being something *other than God.* Only God is eternal, and the creation is temporal. A modern version of pantheism can be found today among radical environmentalists who identify the created world with God.

Zoroastrianism is an ancient religious belief based on the idea that a god by the name of Ahura Mazda created two forces, one good and the other bad. These two forces constantly struggle against each other, and the struggle never ends. The Zoroastrian worldview lies behind many of the video games that young people play.

Genesis also teaches that both good and evil exist, but evil is not eternal, and the struggle is not without end. The good news in the biblical worldview is that God in Christ took for himself the struggle against Satan and sin. Christ and all those who are with him are victorious.

3. The Nature of Human Beings

Human beings are distinct from all the rest of God's creation according to the creation story in Genesis. Humans are made in the image of God. This means that all humans were given the ability to know God, to live with him in a relationship of love and obedience, and to obey his commands (Genesis 1:27).

Humans possess a unique value, therefore, and human life inside or outside the womb should be protected. All humans are one race, regardless of color, tribe, caste, nationality, or gender. Male and female alike are made in the image of God and are equal in value before him.

Therefore, the creation story in Genesis removes all basis for racism, tribalism, sexism, caste, social classism, and nationalism—all of which are produced by sin. The good news of the biblical worldview is that because we all are of one race, we can be saved through one gospel and by one Savior, Jesus Christ, who took to himself our human nature in order to redeem us from our sins.

4. The Reality of Sin and the Way of Salvation

Genesis 3 tells the story of the fall into sin by the first humans, Adam and Eve. Here lies the answer to the question concerning the origin of sin, suffering, and evil in the world. We also face the question that lies at the center of all human cultures: Whom do we serve? Whom do we obey? Adam and Eve chose to obey Satan, the fallen angel, and by their disobedience, sin and the judgment of God came upon the entire world. Human nature and all the cultures humans produce have been corrupted by sin from that time on. Each one runs away from God to serve something, or someone, else.

The good news is that Genesis 3 contains the first missionary call in Scripture and the first revelation of the redemptive purpose of God. Genesis 3:8–9 says that God came looking for our first fallen parents. God called, "Adam, where are you?" God has been calling in a similar way for centuries through prophets and missionaries, and most of all through his Son, Jesus Christ. We see for the first time that God is a *missionary* God in Genesis!

Genesis 3:15 is rightly called the "mother of all gospel promises."

> And I will put enmity between you [the Serpent] and the woman, and between your offspring and hers; he will crush your head, and you will strike his heel.

It is directed to all humanity. Terrible hatred will persist, the verse says, between the two "offsprings," that of the Serpent and that of the woman. Someday, though, the offspring of the woman will come, and he will crush the head of the Serpent (call this the first "birth announcement" of Jesus). Sin, suffering, and judgment are overcome in the worldview of the Bible through Christ, the Savior of the world.

OLD TESTAMENT ISRAEL, A PEOPLE CHOSEN FOR A MISSIONARY PURPOSE

Genesis 1–11 deals with the origin and development of the human race as a whole. This is called a period of "universal-

ism." God chooses Abraham and his descendants to be the objects of his special grace and revelation, and a blessing to all peoples on earth, in Genesis 12:1–3. This began the period of "particularism," in which God worked particularly through one nation, Israel.

Israel was called to be a "missionary nation." The people were to be servants of God, his witnesses, priests, and mediators before the nations (Isaiah 42:5–7; 43:10–13). Israel was to be a living example or "showcase" of the righteous kingdom of God. The nations could learn through the faith and life of Israel and say, "Here are people who know and serve a wonderful God. His laws are fair and benefit everyone. They even protect the animals and preserve the soil. Best of all, these people have *hope,* for by the sacrifices they offer, their God forgives their sins, and they expect a Messiah someday."

The failures of Israel are well known. The people lost much of their witness by adopting elements of pagan religions. They became more concerned with their racial and national identity than with being witnesses for God. They had little concern for lost Gentiles to be saved (see the book of Jonah).

God made sure that Israel became a blessing to the nations despite these failures. Jews received and preserved the Old Testament Scriptures and translated them into Greek, the most widely used language in the days of the apostles. Inspired Jewish writers kept the idea alive that one day all nations and peoples would hear the Word of God and would respond. Christ came out of Israel, and he is the Savior of the world (John 4:42).

The missionary calling was not entirely lost among the Jews. A Jewish mission to the Gentiles had begun in the period before Christ (Matthew 23:15; John 7:35). Jesus' "Great Commission," therefore, did not come as a complete surprise. It had its basis in the history and Scriptures of Israel, going back all the way to Abraham. It is impossible, in fact, to understand missions properly in the New Testament without seeing the roots of missions in the Old Testament.

Review Questions

1. What advice did De Ridder offer?

2. How do you define "worldview"?

3. Identify and explain four basic convictions (worldviews) taught in the Old Testament.

4. In what ways did Israel fulfill its missionary calling?

Discussion Questions

1. Identify at least three psalms that speak of all nations worshipping God.

2. Give three passages from the prophets of the Old Testament that you could use for a message about missions.

3. Was De Ridder correct? Explain.

Chapter 5

Missions in the Four Gospels

The European mission scholar, Johannes Verkuyl, says the following about the New Testament:

> From beginning to end, the New Testament is a book of mission. It owes its very existence to the missionary work of the early Christian churches, both Jewish and Hellenistic. The Gospels are, as it were, "live recordings" of missionary preaching, and the Epistles are not so much some form of missionary apologetic as they are authentic and actual instruments of mission work. (*Contemporary Missiology*, 101–2)

JESUS, THE SAVIOR OF THE WORLD

Everything the Old Testament teaches leads up to the person and work of Jesus of Nazareth. Jesus fulfills the prophecies, hopes, and expectations of the saints of ancient times and opens up the door of heaven to people around the world. Half-gentile Samaritans of the town of Sychar first expressed this truth in words when they said, "This man really is the Savior of the world" (John 4:42).

Jesus went to Nazareth, his hometown, at the beginning of his ministry. He entered the synagogue to worship on the Sabbath. The leaders of the synagogue invited him to read the Scriptures and speak to the people. Jesus read these words from Isaiah 61:1–2:

> The Spirit of the Lord is on me,
>   because he has anointed me
>   to preach good news to the poor.
> He has sent me to proclaim freedom for the prisoners
>   and recovery of sight for the blind,
> to release the oppressed,
>   to proclaim the year of the Lord's favor. (Luke
>   4:18–19)

With the eyes of everyone in the synagogue turned toward him, Jesus added, *"Today this scripture is fulfilled in your hearing"* (Luke 4:18–21).

That moment in the synagogue of Nazareth was the turning point in the redemptive work of God. The mission of Jesus, the One sent by the Father, was begun. The "year of the Lord's favor" to which Jesus referred was the period of time when the gospel was to be preached to all. We will look now at Jesus as the four Gospels describe him. He is the divine Missionary and the one who commissions his followers to preach the gospel to all and to evangelize all peoples of the world.

JESUS THE MISSIONARY

A missionary is a person who is "sent." John 20:21 is a key text for understanding the missionary character of Jesus. Jesus says, "As the Father has sent me, I am sending you." Jesus knew that his heavenly Father had sent him into the world on a mission. The mission was "to seek and to save what was lost" (Luke 19:10). This same Jesus sends believers to go to the ends of the earth making disciples until the end of time (Matthew 28:19–20).

The role of Jesus during his ministry on earth, according to the Gospels, was to *be* the Sent One, and *to make his people missionary*. Jesus' actions throughout his ministry were missionary in character. Jesus showed his passion for lost people and their salvation in his conversations with people like Nicodemus (John 3) and the Samaritan woman (John 4), and by his stories about the lost sheep, the lost coin, and the lost son (Luke 15). The Gospels portray Jesus as the Missionary Messiah.

THE FOUR GOSPELS AS "MISSIONARY LITERATURE"

All four Gospels were written when the church was actively engaged in missions. They were intended to be read by people who needed to know about Jesus, believe in him, and draw others to him as well. Each Gospel tells the story of Jesus to a specific audience.

- Matthew was written for Jews, to teach them about Jesus and make them support missions to Gentiles.
- Mark was a missionary "tract" for Gentiles who needed a brief account of the life and teachings of Jesus.
- Luke, a gentile convert to faith in Jesus, wrote for Gentiles like himself who needed to know that Jesus wanted Gentiles as well as Jews in his kingdom.
- John openly declared his missionary purpose: "that you may believe that Jesus is the Christ, the Son of God, and that by believing you may have life in his name" (John 20:31). John addressed the world. The book of John presents a series of evangelistic conversations between Jesus and others, conversations that have led many people around the world to faith in Christ.

Jesus' Mission on Earth

We must look at Jesus and the nature of his mission on earth to understand missions. We see that the Son of God became incarnate, taking our flesh and blood and living like us in everything except sin. *Compassion* could be seen in his entire mission. Jesus cared deeply for the sick, the hungry, and people who mourned. He demonstrated his power over Satan by many miracles. He spent time with sinners of various kinds.

His ministry was mainly to *preach and teach* the message of the kingdom. He *sacrificed himself* for sinners all the way to the cross. He rose from the dead, demonstrated his authority, commanded his followers to carry the news of his lordship to the world, and ascended to heaven. There he reigns until he will come to earth again.

The proclamation of the kingdom of Christ is a missionary command for people who follow other lords and saviors to cut their ties and submit their hearts and lives to the Lord Jesus alone. Missionary proclamation is an urgent matter. It asks for total surrender and radical change. It is not a theory to be discussed but an announcement to be made. It is an invitation to lost people to enter the house of God and be saved.

Teachings About Missions in the Stories Jesus Told

Jesus told many stories when he preached and these stories contain important teachings about missions. For example, in the story of the harvest (Matthew 9:37–38), Jesus challenged his followers to open their eyes to the great size of the harvest waiting for reapers. Jesus told them to pray to the Lord to whom the harvest belongs, to send workers into this great harvest.

Luke 15 contains the stories of the three lost things—the sheep, the coin, and the son. Jesus told these stories in response to the religious leaders who criticized him for talking to the "outcasts" of society. This is the lesson taught in all three stories: God wants lost people found, and heaven rejoices when sinners repent and come home. The missionary message is plain to see.

Jesus taught us what to expect in missions in the story of the four soils (Matthew 13:1–23). The word of the gospel is brought to people who are resistant, to others who show temporary interest, to others who bear no fruit, and (thank God!) to others who are receptive and fruitful. This story has given fresh insight and courage to evangelists and missionaries as they confront these four kinds of "soil" among people.

Joel F. Williams offers the following insights into the story of the sower and what it teaches about the sovereignty of God in the work of missions:

> One of the odd features of Jesus' parable is that the sower is apparently a wasteful farmer. Without a great deal of concern, the sower throws seeds along the road, on rocks, among thorns, as well as on good soil. The common practice at that time of plowing after sowing may partially explain the sower's actions. Also, some loss is simply the typical condition of farming. Yet the abundant harvest is clearly the result of God's blessing and not the sower's skill. The size of the harvest is out of proportion to the ability of the sower. Jesus tells a similar parable about a sower who scatters seeds and then goes to sleep, only to find later that the seeds sprout and grow all on their own without his help (Mark 4:24–30). An underlying principle that helps us to make sense of both parables is that ultimately the harvest is the work of God.
>
> This is God's mission. He sends, he empowers, and he produces the results. The ultimate purpose for the mission is to bring glory to God, so that a multitude from every nation, tribe, people and language might declare the praise and honor and glory and power of

God for all eternity. Believers participate in God's mission not because God needs their contribution but because they have convictions concerning the importance of God and his will and because God in his grace stooped to include human agents in the accomplishment of his work. God stands at the center of mission as it is described in the New Testament. (William J. Larkin, Jr., and Joel F. Williams, *Mission in the New Testament*, 239–40)

THE CROSS, RESURRECTION, AND GREAT COMMISSION OF CHRIST

Jesus suffered the judgment of God in our place on the cross. He suffered, once and for all, for Israel and the Gentiles. His resurrection likewise, meant victory over Satan, death, and judgment for the whole worldwide community of believers. The cross and resurrection of Jesus is the basis for the Christian mission. It is not surprising, therefore, that we find reports of his cross and resurrection together with commands to carry the gospel to all peoples.

Each of the four Gospels ends with a "Great Commission" after telling the story of Christ's death and resurrection. Jesus says that his will is that his disciples take the gospel to all peoples everywhere. The four passages are

- Matthew 28:18–20
- Mark 16:15–18
- Luke 24:44–48
- John 20:21–23

The roots of these missionary commands are found in Old Testament passages like Genesis 12:3; 15:5; and Isaiah 49:6. Christ indicates that his personal ministry on earth is now finished and the "end time" is about to begin by way of these final instructions before his ascension. Now the Old Testament prophecies regarding the gathering of the nations will be fulfilled.

The heart of all the commission texts is *Make people everywhere followers of me*. Following Jesus means (1) believing in him alone as your Savior; (2) obeying him as your Lord and King of your life; and, (3) carrying out his missionary command to make disciples of all peoples. The calling and destiny of Israel are now fulfilled in Jesus whose arms are open to all nations, peoples, and races. He is the door into the kingdom, and no one who comes to him will be turned away.

REVIEW QUESTIONS

1. Explain the significance of Jesus' message in the synagogue in Nazareth.

2. What does it mean that Jesus is the "Missionary Messiah"?

3. To what particular audience does each of the four Gospels speak?

4. Quote the four "Great Commission" texts.

DISCUSSION QUESTIONS

1. How would you describe the "kingdom of God"?

2. Compare the four "Great Commission" texts and identify the special elements in each one.

3. How do we explain the sovereignty of God in missions and our responsibility to take the gospel to all peoples in light of what Joel F. Williams says about the parable of the sower?

4. Discuss some of the other parables Jesus told and how they teach us about missions.

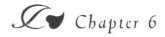 *Chapter 6*

Missions in Acts and the Epistles

In this chapter we will examine the social context in which the early missionaries and evangelists worked, the opposition they encountered, and some of their methods. We will examine closely the methods used by the apostle Paul in a later chapter.

We always keep in mind that *divine* activities lie behind the *human* activities required in missions. Mission activity is first and foremost the work of the triune God. William J. Larkin, Jr., reminds us,

> It is common to recognize that Luke's presentation of mission in Acts is less about the "Acts of the Apostles" than about the "Acts of the Holy Spirit," less about the mission of the church than about the mission of God. Detailed study reveals how true these characterizations are. For Luke's narrative portrays each person of the Godhead as a "sending one," both in commissioning and promoting mission. Each person of the Trinity is also a "sent one," a direct agent of mission, as well as a participant working through human agents. Finally, Luke does not hesitate to emphasize that the results of mission are divine results. (*Mission in the New Testament*, 174–75)

Larkin is correct when he affirms that the triune God is the author, source of power, and director of missions. Missions represents an undertaking far beyond human capability. In the end, therefore, the results of missions are due to the sovereign grace of God, and all glory must go to him. We keep this in mind as we focus attention on the work of the human agents of missions and the conditions they have confronted.

THE SOCIAL CONTEXT OF MISSIONS

No period in world history was better suited to the growth of the church than the first century A.D. The Roman Empire controlled much of the world. This brought peace, unity, safety in travel, and stable government to millions of people. The widespread use of the Greek language made communication fairly easy.

Despite the strength of Rome, however, there were signs of decay throughout society. Many people felt insecure and uncertain about the future. Old beliefs and ideas in religion and philosophy were losing their attraction. People were looking for new ideas, a better religion than they had known in the past, and a stronger basis for a moral society. Religious cults and "mystery" religions multiplied in this context.

Jews were scattered throughout the Roman world and synagogues could be found in many cities. The Hebrew Bible was available in the Greek language. Monotheism, the Jewish belief in one God, attracted people who saw the moral laws of the Hebrew Scriptures as offering a better basis for society than the religions of the Greeks and the Romans. Jewish missionaries also actively promoted the beliefs and moral values of Judaism.

OPPOSITION TO CHRISTIAN MISSIONS

1. Opposition from the Jews

The book of Acts tells us that Jewish religious leaders opposed Christianity from the start. The crucial question for the Jews was *Who was Jesus?* Was he the Messiah promised in the

Scriptures? Was he more than a great prophet? How did his death on the cross fit into expectations of the Messiah?

The Jews in general despised the message of a crucified Messiah whom the Christians identified with the God of the Bible. Jews saw that as the Christian faith spread among Gentiles, converts did not keep the laws of Moses, especially the requirement of circumcision. Furthermore, the spread of the Christian faith irritated other Gentiles, and in some cases Jews were blamed. Jewish leaders viewed Christian missions as a threat to their security, and on this basis they opposed it.

Christians still hoped to win the people of Israel during the first century. The division between Judaism and Christianity became so deep by the end of the first century that missions to Jews almost became impossible. It was one of the early failures of Christian missions that it did not win many Jews.

2. *Opposition from the Gentiles*

The Gentiles opposed the spread of the gospel for a number of reasons.

a. *Gentiles viewed Christianity as causing divisions and as being harmful to society.* Gentiles tolerated all kinds of religions and cults, but they persecuted Christians. Gentiles believed the evil rumors that were spread about Christians. They regarded Christians as traitors because they refused to worship the Roman emperor. Christians also refused to participate in certain immoral sports that the Gentiles enjoyed.

b. *Gentiles regarded Christianity as being too new to be true, and both intellectually and culturally inferior.* The message of the cross and of salvation by faith in Jesus was ridiculous to the Gentiles. Furthermore, many of the early Christians were poor and uneducated, and some were slaves. Gentiles looked down on them and opposed the spread of their religion.

c. *Christians insisted that there was only one God, who alone was to be worshipped, and one Savior, the Lord Jesus Christ.* The Romans rejected such a "narrow" religion and the strict moral teachings that came with it. They were angered especially by Christians refusing to recognize the emperor as "god."

MISSIONARY APPROACHES

1. One Gospel and Many "Translations"

The early Christians had to "translate" the words and ideas of the gospel into languages and practices that all kinds of people could understand as they began to carry the gospel to the world. This "translation" was a dangerous task because in the process the gospel itself might be changed or lost. Yet it had to be done in order to move the gospel from the Jewish community and its traditions to the peoples and cultures of the world.

Evangelists and missionaries brought the gospel to slaves and free, men and women, intellectuals and the uneducated, astrologers and superstitious people, and followers of other religions. Each of these groups represented a particular challenge. They all needed to hear the gospel in ways they could grasp and in languages they understood. This was an enormous task, filled with risks and requiring great knowledge, insight, and spiritual wisdom.

The apostles used a variety of approaches, but they never changed the basic truths of the gospel. The sermons recorded in Acts and the teachings contained in the Epistles illustrate this fact. They proclaimed faith in one God, who sent the one Savior, Jesus, to die for sinners. They told of the resurrection from the dead and the hope of the return of Christ. They attacked immorality, which was considered closely connected to idolatry. They expected no improvement in human conduct without repentance and conversion to faith in Jesus Christ.

2. Insistence on Conversion to Jesus Christ

The early missionaries insisted that all those who wished to become disciples of Christ be *converted*. This meant believing in Christ alone as their Savior and Lord, abandoning all other gods and religious practices, and changing their manner of living in order to conform to the teachings of Christ.

This kind of religious conversion was foreign to the world of the first century. People did not feel that it was necessary to give up one set of religious ideas in order to adopt another. They did not see the connection between religious beliefs and moral practices. They did not like it that Christians insisted that they should hold right beliefs about Christ in order to be saved.

The early missionaries insisted that conversion was necessary even though the Christian idea of conversion to Christ was not popular. They would not compromise. Missions aimed at conversion. They would not settle for some form of dialogue that ended with everyone retaining his or her own religion. The message they preached was all about Jesus Christ.

The missionaries were confident that when the message was believed, it became a life-changing force in the hearts of people and in society. Once people were converted, a new foundation for life was laid. Their social and cultural interests began to change under the influence of the Holy Spirit, and the love of God in Christ moved them to seek righteousness in one relationship after another. They began to serve their fellow human beings. Missions claims the same things today.

Acts and the Epistles teach us that we must keep the right order. First, there must be conversion from idolatry to faith in the one true God revealed in Jesus Christ. This is followed by baptism, the disciplines of Christian discipleship, and active membership in the family of believers. If you change the order, you cut off the source of life-changing power. As Michael Green expressed it years ago,

> Once you sever the fundamental root of conversion to Christ from the Christian message, it becomes a broken and a lifeless plant, however beautiful the flowers of concern and social involvement it displays. (*Evangelism in the Early Church*, 148)

3. Some Full-Time Professionals and Many Lay Missionaries

Acts and the Epistles tell us of the work of full-time "professionals," such as Paul, Silas, Barnabas, Timothy, Titus, and others. There were also many other traveling missionaries sent out by the churches and supported by the gifts and services of faithful believers. These lay missionaries made up the largest group of early ambassadors of the gospel.

Women as well as men were involved. Examine how many women are among Paul's "co-workers" in the gospel whom he greets in Romans 16! These women ministered to the churches that met in their homes; they prophesied, spoke in tongues, corrected and instructed ill-informed evangelists like Apollos, and served as deaconesses.

Acts and the Epistles give us the picture of an ample number of people that formally and informally engaged in spreading the gospel. People from all parts of society filled the ranks of witnesses. They witnessed to Christ by their transformed lives, their verbal witnessing, sacrificial service, and the loving fellowship of the church. All the things for which Paul prayed in his epistles to the churches contributed to the witness of the church. Put this all together, and you see the picture of the Body of Christ serving as a lighthouse of faith, hope, and love in a decaying Roman society.

4. Many Different Methods

The New Testament says nothing about many things that are common today. One example is the church building. No special church buildings were used for the first two hundred years. There was a great deal of preaching, but no mention of formal "sermons" or pulpits. Believers preached in synagogues, in the open air, in private homes, and in rented buildings. Any place was good enough if people could be gathered to hear the gospel.

Moral living was a major emphasis of the apostles, along with doctrine. They made no division between right faith and right conduct. Both came under the authority of Christ and his Word.

Prayer was a primary instrument in the early missions. It began on the Day of Pentecost, when a prayer meeting became the occasion for the outpouring of the Holy Spirit and a great evangelistic meeting. Prayer became a basic method of breaking down Satan's strongholds and establishing the church of Christ.

Along with prayer, the Scriptures were the apostles' second basic instrument. They used the Septuagint, the Greek translation of the Old Testament, as their source of truth and authority in preaching. The early missionaries set out to evangelize the world, moved and accompanied by love for people and zeal to bring glory to God by drawing people to worship him. The quality of their living, speaking, and dying witnessed to their exalted Lord.

REVIEW QUESTIONS

1. Describe the social context of early missions.

2. Explain why (a) Jews and (b) Gentiles opposed missions.

3. Identify and explain four methods that missionaries used.

4. What roles did lay men and lay women play in missions?

DISCUSSION QUESTIONS

1. Describe the social context of missions in your country and in one other country where mission work is needed.

2. What are three common objections to the gospel today?

3. What can we learn from missions in New Testament times?

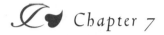 *Chapter 7*

The Holy Spirit
and Missions

Where can Jesus' followers ever find the strength and resources to bring the gospel to so many people, in so many places, and in the face of so much opposition? Jesus gave the answer shortly before he returned to heaven.

> You will receive power when the Holy Spirit comes on you; and you will be my witnesses in Jerusalem, and in all Judea and Samaria, and to the ends of the earth. (Acts 1:8)

Harry R. Boer, who served as a missionary in Nigeria for many years, said the following about this verse:

> The words, "You shall BE my witnesses" do not merely state what the Church would DO, but what the Church would BE. The Great Commission, as the divine mandate to the Church to be a witnessing Church, is not only a law similar to that which was set forth at the beginning of human history ("be fruitful and multiply"), but it is its spiritual counterpart in the new creation. It is a statement of the task of the renewed humanity as the earlier statement expresses the task of the old hu-

manity. The urge to witness is inborn in the Church. It is given with her very being. She cannot not-witness. She has this being because of the Spirit who indwells her. *Pentecost made the Church a witnessing Church because at Pentecost the witnessing Spirit identified Himself with the Church and made the Great Commission the law of her life.* (*Pentecost and Missions,* 122–23, my italics)

Here we have the two important ideas. The Bible reveals the person and work of the Spirit as being intensely missionary in character and purpose. The Spirit is a *missionary* Spirit who desires to bring home the lost children of God. The church immediately became a *missionary* church in its very being when it experienced the baptism of the Holy Spirit at Pentecost. The Holy Spirit and missions cannot be separated from Pentecost on.

THE WORK OF THE MISSIONARY SPIRIT IN BELIEVERS

The Holy Spirit, first of all, *awakens an interest in missions in the hearts of believers.* Missionary zeal, at its deepest level, is a holy jealousy for the honor and glory of Jesus Christ. It may be called the "patriotism of the kingdom of Christ." The thought that millions of people worship false gods and care nothing for Jesus Christ is deeply disturbing to Spirit-filled Christians. We want all people everywhere to worship the one true God, and missions is the means by which we seek to bring it about.

Second, the Holy Spirit *plants in the minds of believers a compassion for people who are perishing.* You find Christians looking at the world with burning hearts whenever the Spirit is freely at work. God's concern for lost sinners becomes more and more the burden of Spirit-filled believers. They look for new and better ways to communicate the gospel to people everywhere.

That is why whenever the church experiences revival, renewed interest is shown in evangelism and missions.

Third, the Holy Spirit *builds faith in God's promise that the proclamation of the gospel will not be in vain.* Without that faith, evangelizing the world is an impossible dream. The promise that the Word of God will not return to him empty (Isaiah 55:11) takes hold of us with Spirit-given faith, and we look for ways to act on God's promise.

Fourth, the Holy Spirit *creates in the believer the willingness to obey Christ's missionary command.* Spirit-generated obedience can take you to the ends of the earth and cause you to endure the most awful conditions.

Men and women risk death for the honor and freedom of their country in times of war. Why is it that so few Christians will risk their health and lives for the honor and kingdom of Christ? Pray that the Holy Spirit will plant within us and many others a *willingness* to do the will of God in missions at whatever cost.

Fifth, the Holy Spirit *breaks down our social and racial prejudices and makes us love people who are different and welcome them into the kingdom of Jesus Christ.* The book of Acts tells us a great deal about the social and racial prejudices among the first believers. All the missionary witness of the church up to Acts 10 was limited to people who belonged to the broader Jewish community. The city of Samaria where Philip evangelized, for example, was not gentile territory, and the Ethiopian whom Philip met was religiously related to the Jews as a "God-fearer."

In Acts 10, however, we see that the Holy Spirit taught Peter and the church that they had to overcome their prejudices, put an end to separations, and welcome Gentiles into the community of believers. The "gentile Pentecost" described in Acts 10:44–46 changed the character of the church. Church doors were thrown open to everybody from that point on.

The church most needs another "Pentecost" of the kind that happened at Cornelius's home, when social and racial barriers were removed by the baptism of the Holy Spirit. Racism, tribalism, nationalism, and differences of social class not only keep Christians apart, to our disgrace, but they prevent the spread of the gospel. Emotional appeals and arguments cannot take away prejudices that are rooted deep in the heart and have been there for years. Only the Holy Spirit can! Pray for the kind of "Pentecost" that will put an end to our separations!

THE SPECIAL WORK OF THE SPIRIT IN MISSIONS

People who leave houses, brothers, sisters, father, mother, children, and country for the sake of Christ and the gospel receive from him special promises and rewards (Matthew 19:29). One of the greatest is the *spiritual bond between missionaries and Christians in other lands and with supporters of missions everywhere.* The Holy Spirit is the one who draws them together in the "fellowship of the Great Commission."

This fellowship consists of men and women, churches and organizations that work, sacrifice, and pray for the spread of the gospel. The bond between Christians who have hearts for missions is one of the most precious experiences on earth. Whenever missionaries meet other missionaries, they immediately feel that they are "family." When those who "go" meet those who "send and support," the missionary Spirit unites them around common interests and purpose.

Second, the Holy Spirit *opens doors for the gospel.* Paul writes in 1 Corinthians 16:8–9 about the "open door" of mission opportunity that he found in an unexpected place, the big and wicked city of Ephesus. The history of missions is filled with stories of doors being opened that nobody expected ever would move. The great "Door Opener," the Holy Spirit, is sovereign and almighty. Neither the hardness of an individual heart nor the stubborn resistance of an entire city or nation can resist him when he chooses to move.

Third, the Holy Spirit *prepares the hearts of unbelievers to desire what Christ offers, to inquire about the Christian faith, and to convict them of their sin and their need for salvation.* Jesus said that it is the task of the Spirit to "convict the world of guilt in regard to sin and righteousness and judgment" (John 16:8).

The work of the Holy Spirit—convicting sinners that they need a savior, planting new life in hearts dead in sin, and giving faith in Christ—is an absolute requirement for the success of missions. The voices of evangelists and missionaries can penetrate no deeper than the eardrums. Only God can go inside and speak to the heart, and that is the unique work of the Spirit.

Fourth, the Holy Spirit *preserves and nourishes the fruit of missions.* Paul expresses this clearly when he writes to the church he had planted in the city of Philippi.

> In all my prayers for all of you, I always pray with joy because of your partnership in the gospel from the first day until now, *being confident of this, that he [God the Holy Spirit] who began a good work in you will carry it on to completion until the day of Christ Jesus.* (Philippians 1:4–6)

Because the Holy Spirit abides forever, God's harvest will not be lost (John 14:16). Mission efforts will not be in vain, nor will the labors and sacrifices of God's servants be forgotten. There are sure to be temporary setbacks and severe disappointments. The prophet Isaiah also experienced the force of opposition, yet he spoke with confidence and optimism about the proclamation of the Word of God.

> Instead of the thornbush will grow the pine tree,
> and instead of briers the myrtle will grow.

This will be for the LORD's renown,
for an everlasting sign,
which will not be destroyed. (Isaiah 55:13)

THE GIFTS OF THE SPIRIT FOR THE MINISTRIES THAT GOD DESIRES

Roland Allen was a missionary to China in the early part of the twentieth century. He offered two important words of advice.

(1) Trust the Holy Spirit to equip and guide the church in every place without continual dependence on outside leaders and financial resources.

(2) Trust local believers, including young Christians, to learn from the Word of God, do what is right, and manage the affairs of the church without outsiders telling them what they should do.[1]

Roland Allen learned these mission principles from the apostle Paul, who made the churches he planted dependent not on him but on God the Holy Spirit. Hardly anything is more important for missionary policy today than following Paul's practice in teaching converts and congregations to depend on the spiritual gifts, wisdom, and resources of the Holy Spirit (1 Corinthians 12–14).

Dependency on outsider leaders is damaging churches in many places. Missionaries who want to control the churches sometimes cause this dependency. At other times the cause lies with local believers who have not learned to give generously to the Lord's work. They prefer to let other people provide the resources. Dependency on outsiders is very often due to a lack

---

1 Allen's best known books are *Missionary Methods: St. Paul's or Ours?* and *The Spontaneous Expansion of the Church.*

of trust in the Holy Spirit's ability to provide spiritually and ma-
terially for every ministry that is God's will and has his blessing.

WHAT ABOUT THE HARD PLACES?

Indeed, there are hard places, where the "soil" of people's
hearts is very resistant to the gospel and mission work hardly
makes any progress. Most people in such places will not listen
at all. Others show interest for a while, but then turn away. This
is exactly what Jesus predicted would happen when he told the
story of the sower (Matthew 13:1–23). Jesus identifies Satan as
the "evil one" who sets up barriers to the gospel and prevents
people from hearing and responding to the Word of God.

There are many examples of hard places today. Resistance
to the gospel is strong among Muslims and Jews. Opposition is
growing among Buddhists and Hindus. What can missionaries
do when most of the "soil" in the fields where they work is resistant or full of thorns?

*Like the sower in the story, be patient, continue sowing, and re-
member the Holy Spirit!* The special assignment of the Holy Spirit
is to change hard ground into "good soil." He will deal with the
weeds and briers in his own time. He will cause beautiful plants
and trees to grow in their place to the praise of the name of
God (Isaiah 55:13).

Perganum was a first-century city that was so bad that Jesus
described it as a place "where Satan has his throne" and "where
Satan lives" (Revelation 2:12–13). Yet, missionaries planted a
church in Perganum, and the believers remained true to
Christ despite bloody persecution (verse 13). Their witness to
Jesus was "unto death," the blood-witness of suffering and mar-
tyrdom. The strength they required came from the source of
all power, the Holy Spirit.

Hard places like Perganum are increasing in number in
the world. Missionaries need to learn from the start, and keep
learning throughout their ministries, to trust in the Holy

Spirit. The Spirit sustained the Lord Jesus all the way to Calvary, and he will sustain us in every situation.

Review Questions

1. What does it mean to call the Holy Spirit the missionary Spirit?

2. Identify five ways the Spirit inspires believers to missions.

3. What does the Spirit do for missionaries and their work?

Discussion Questions

1. Where are the really "hard" places today?

2. How "racist" or "separatist" is your church?

3. Why do you think the advice of Roland Allen is still important?

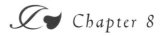 Chapter 8

The Missionary Methods of the Apostle Paul

The primary method that the apostle Paul used to communicate the gospel of Jesus Christ was by word of mouth. Paul believed that the spoken word is the primary way that the Holy Spirit inspires faith in the hearts of those who hear. Romans 10:17 sums up what the apostle believed about this: "Faith comes from hearing the message, and the message is heard through the word of Christ."

Paul set out to tell the message of the gospel of Christ on this basis to as many people as he could reach. He spelled out this message in the opening verses of his letter to the Romans.

First, the gospel is *of God* (Romans 1:1b), meaning that the gospel comes from God, not from humans. The proclamation of the gospel is the result of God's eternal and sovereign purpose.

Second, the gospel was *promised many years before by the prophets of the Old Testament* (Romans 1:2–3a). The gospel is the good news of the gift of God's righteousness to sinners who believe in Jesus Christ. The gospel plainly presented in the New Testament is rooted in the promises of the Old Testament.

Third, the gospel is *all about Jesus Christ,* who was a descendant of King David according to his human nature and declared with power to be the eternal Son of God by his resurrection from the dead (Romans 1:3–4).

Fourth, the proclamation of the gospel is *for all peoples everywhere* (Romans 1:5). Paul was eager to preach the gospel in the great city of Rome with all its different races, cultures, and religions because he knew the gospel was "the power of God for the salvation of everyone who believes" (Romans 1:16).

Paul summarized his primary method and the reason behind it in his first letter to the church at Corinth. Paul wrote, "We preach Christ crucified: a stumbling block to Jews and foolishness to Gentiles, but to those whom God has called, both Jews and Greeks, Christ the power of God and the wisdom of God" (1 Corinthians 1:23–24).

All of Paul's missionary activities fit within his overall plan to advance God's kingdom. He began with winning disciples by evangelism and gathering them into churches. Paul continued this strategy by strengthening young churches so that through them wider communities might be transformed by the power of the gospel. The method was successful. As history shows, the gospel spread everywhere and eventually affected the entire Roman Empire.

KEY METHODS THAT PAUL USED

1. Paul confronted people with the saviorhood and lordship of Christ and urged them to submit their hearts and lives to him.

This was based on Paul's own conversion experience (Acts 9:1–9). When he was confronted with the reality that Jesus was alive and reigning in heaven, his entire way of thinking had to change. He had to give himself completely to Jesus Christ.

Paul was aware of the hardness of an unconverted human heart and its resistance to the divine way of salvation (Romans 3:10–18). He also knew that abandoning traditional religions was not a popular idea in his day. It was not acceptable to insist on only one God and one Savior. Yet Paul refused to make conversion to Christ an easy thing to do. He sought to win *disciples* of Christ, not nominal converts who still held onto old religious beliefs.

So Paul insisted that those who wanted to come to Christ repent from sin and every form of idolatry. They had to change their whole way of thinking about religion, as Paul did when Christ took hold of him (Philippians 3:7–9). They also had to submit completely to the lordship of Christ over their daily lives. There was no other way into the kingdom of God.

2. Paul focused on families and households in both evangelism and outreach into society.

Paul focused mainly on families and family relationships. He assumed that once the gospel took root in a home and among family members it would eventually make an impact on the entire community.

The "families" and "households" of Paul's time were similar to the "extended" families that are common in many parts of the world today. When the New Testament speaks of a family or household (1 Corinthians 1:16; Galatians 6:10), it refers to more than one set of parents with their children. It includes everyone living together and related to one another, plus friends, servants, and even neighbors and guests in their homes.

Paul made his first converts in the environment of the home nearly everywhere he preached. The converts were baptized together and shared the Holy Communion together. The first blows against racial and social discrimination, and against slavery and mistreatment of women, were struck at the Communion table where Jew and Gentile, master and slave, men and women sat together around the same table and confessed their dependence on the same Savior.

It was Paul's strategy to preach the gospel, win converts, and teach the first and basic lessons in the context of the extended family. These lessons concerned the nature of the church as the family of God and the transforming life of the kingdom. Thank God, this continues to happen in many places throughout the world.

3. Paul stressed the importance of planting and nurturing churches and communities of faith, worship, fellowship, and service.

Paul was never satisfied with merely making individual disciples. He gathered and organized disciples into churches with local spiritual leaders wherever he could (1 Timothy 3; Titus 1:5–9). Paul did this because he believed that Christ established the church for an important purpose. Every church was to be a lighthouse and a showcase of the kingdom of God.

Paul established churches in the four Roman provinces of Galatia, Macedonia, Achaia, and Asia within a period of ten years. He hoped to go to Spain, the farthest western side of the empire (Romans 15:24, 28). It is even possible that he got there. Everywhere Paul went he preached, gathered converts, and organized them into local, self-governing churches. His approach was based on the kingdom vision of communities of people who worshipped the one true God and served him in their lives. Such communities were agents of spiritual and social change in towns, cities, and nations.

4. Paul concentrated on developing local leaders in the churches and placing them in charge as soon as possible.

Paul and his companions established churches in many places in the course of their mission journeys. They concentrated on developing local Christian leaders in these churches. Therefore, the apostles did not leave the churches with no one to preach, no one to teach, no one to baptize, and no one to administer the Holy Communion when they departed. The churches also did not have to wait weeks or months for an apostle to visit them again before they could function as churches.

Paul knew that the Holy Spirit gave spiritual gifts to believers for the welfare and ministry of the church (1 Corinthians 12–14). Therefore, Paul prepared local people to teach, preach, minister to the poor, deal with problems, and govern the affairs of the church according to the spiritual gifts that the Holy Spirit distributed among believers. They were not dependent on Christians from outside for fi nances, vital church ministries, or leaders. This method of equipping local leaders and trusting the Holy Spirit to instruct, empower, and guide them, continues to be a vital key to successful mission.

5. Paul used the natural "bridges" of family relatives, friends, and other contacts in spreading the gospel.

Paul traveled from city to city in the first century, following up on his contacts with relatives and friends of Jewish Christians from Antioch and elsewhere. Personal relations were his bridges. Paul used human bridges to carry the gospel to the Jews who lived in many cities, and beyond the Jews to the Gentiles. This insight into *how* he carried out the commission that God had given him was one of the secrets of Paul's success as a missionary.

This method has great potential for mission work today. Cities, towns, and villages are filled with natural human bridges. The gospel can pass over these bridges from person to person and from family to family. The lines of family and friendship run from city to village and back again and across the cities. This makes human networks as important in spreading the gospel today as they were in the first century.

6. Paul started "house churches" everywhere he went. These house churches became living cells of the Body of Christ. Paul used a large number of "fellow workers" (called "lay people" today) to spread the gospel and minister in the house churches.

When Paul said, "I am obligated both to Greeks and non-Greeks, both to the wise and the foolish" (Romans 1:14), he was stating a principle that applied not only to himself but to every believer. Conversion meant enlistment in the army of Jesus Christ. Paul considered personal witnessing and service to neighbors in need to be a natural part of citizenship in the kingdom of Jesus Christ.

Likewise, Paul enlisted a wide circle of co-workers, "lay" men and women, in the planting of churches where believers could gather for worship, fellowship, instruction, and service to persons in need. Missionaries today can learn a great deal about *how* the early apostles passed on their own zeal for missions to others by examining Romans 16. Paul mentions a great number of his "fellow workers" by name, both men and women. We find a key to the early spread of the gospel in this list of workers: *conversion was followed by service, and missions involved everybody.*

J. H. Bavinck was a Dutch mission scholar and a former missionary to Indonesia. Bavinck was impressed by the repeated references in the book of Acts and the epistles of Paul to the role played by lay preachers. Bavinck wrote,

> We gain the impression that an intense role was played in the missionary activity of the early church by many men and women who held no other office than that of a believer. To the extent that these lay preachers were on their own, they were in danger of becoming involved in all sorts of confusion, and as a matter of fact this is just what happened. It is however, the great strength of Paul that he did not suppress this spontaneous spreading of the gospel, but utilized and organized it instead. (*An Introduction to the Science of Missions*, 40)

These early lay preachers "held no other office than that of believer." What more did they need in order to tell their neighbors about Christ? History shows that lay men and women, when they are set free from too much work inside the church, can spread the gospel in ways that few clergy can equal.

7. *Paul taught believers to promote justice, truth, and mercy in society and to care for the Lord's earth.*

Paul's mission approach moved from winning converts, to establishing churches, to the community beyond the church, and even on to the care of the earth, the air, and the water God gives us. There is a breadth in Paul's approach that can only be explained by the fact that Paul deeply understood the nature of Christ's authority here and now over heaven and earth (Matthew 28:18).

Paul could hardly mention Jesus Christ without calling him "Lord." He meant by this a lordship that affects the whole way that Christians live. Christ is Lord now, as well as at the end of the age. Since Christ is Lord, and truth, love, and righteousness characterize his rule, his people must practice and promote justice, mercy, and truth in every area of life and be stewards of the earth.

Some missionaries in the past failed because of their limited understanding of the role of the local church in society. Missionaries established churches, but often the churches were indifferent to corruption and injustice in society. Churches failed in their calling to be light, salt, and leaven in a sinful world (Matthew 5:13–16). As a result many people today are disappointed with the gospel. They condemn it for doing so little to transform society and turn away.

The world needs churches whose members are agents of transformation in every area of life. Multitudes need to hear that *Christ is Savior, and He is Lord!* Churches must teach the whole Word of God and a kingdom perspective on life. Christians should learn in the churches about the kingdom of truth and righteousness in which Christ reigns and about their responsibility to bear witness to truth and righteousness in the community, the markets, and the centers of power. *Such churches are the only hope of the world!*

.

REVIEW QUESTIONS

1. What was Paul's primary means of spreading the gospel?

2. Identify and explain four essential elements of the gospel.

3. List and explain the seven key mission methods that Paul used.

DISCUSSION QUESTIONS

1. What additional methods did Paul use in spreading the gospel?

2. How effective do you think these methods are today?

3. Suggest some methods that might serve us well today.

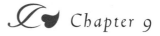 Chapter 9

The Gospel and Other Religions

What do we say about other religions with their teachers, their sacred books, and the gods they worship? By what authority do Christians proclaim the gospel to followers of other faiths and seek to win them to faith in Christ alone?

Followers of other religions say that Christians have no right to claim that the Christian faith is the only true religion. They point to the moral failures of Western countries as evidence of the weakness of Christianity. They say we should stop all evangelism for the sake of peace and harmony in the world. They tell us we should "dialogue" instead of doing mission work. *To dialogue* means to talk to one another about similarities and differences. They say that if we would dialogue instead of evangelize, we would promote understanding, tolerance, and mutual acceptance among followers of all religions.

What should the Christian's attitude be toward the other religions? Are they totally false in every respect, or do they contain some truth? Do their followers worship the same God that Christians worship? Do their sacred books tell the truth about salvation? J. H. Bavinck wrote, "The whole character of the missionary's message is determined by his attitude toward the non-Christian religion that he has to wrestle with" (*The Impact of Christianity on the Non-Christian World*, 109).

OTHER RELIGIONS IN THE LIGHT OF THE BIBLE

Missionaries can only be certain that they have the right attitude toward other religions by studying what the Bible says about them. The Bible, the Old Testament as well as the New, is our authority on all important matters. Jesus and the writers of the New Testament accepted the Old Testament as the Word of God. Their attitude toward non-Christian religions was based on what God revealed in the Old Testament.

1. The Old Testament Teaching

A basic distinction in Old Testament times was between "the nations" and "the people of the covenant." "Covenant" means the special relationship that God made with Abraham and his descendants (Genesis 12:1–3; 17:1–9). People of the covenant were the descendants of Abraham. They became known as the people of Israel. They were called a "holy" people because they were set apart by God as his special possession (Exodus 19:5–6).

Besides the people of Israel, there were "the nations" or "the peoples." These nations were also called "the heathen" and "Gentiles." They had other religions, and they did not live under the covenant given by God to Israel.

God promised to preserve Abraham and his descendants, protect them, and prosper them as long as they kept the covenant he established with them (Genesis 17:1–9). The covenant lay at the center of Israel's life. The religion of the covenant was

- *monotheistic:* the people of the covenant worshipped and served the one God and him only;
- *according to the book:* the people of the covenant believed the writings of Moses, the Psalms, and the Prophets as the authoritative scriptures from which they learned who God was and how he was to be worshipped and obeyed;

- *based on the grace of God:* the people of the covenant lived by trusting in God and his promises;
- *exclusive:* the religions of the other nations were false religions and their gods were idols;
- *a light to the nations:* by the witness of the people of the covenant, the nations would be blessed by learning who the true God is and how he should be worshipped and served (Genesis 18:18–19).

The people of Israel repeatedly failed to keep the covenant, and they worshipped the gods of other nations. Many times God had to say to them, "Get rid of the foreign gods you have with you" (Genesis 35:2). Nevertheless, the Old Testament gave one clear message: The worship of the God of the covenant excluded all other religions with their gods and practices.

Many passages from the Old Testament testify to what we have said. Look at Exodus 20:1–6, 22–23 and Deuteronomy 32:16–18 in the writings of Moses. Listen to Psalms 115:4–8 and 135:15–18. Read Isaiah 41:21–24; 44:6–20; and Jeremiah 10:1–16 from the prophets.

2. The New Testament Teaching

The human authors of the New Testament knew the Old Testament well. Their attitude toward the non-Christian religions was based on their understanding of the Old Testament. It is the urgent task of Christians today to search the Scriptures in order to gain a clear understanding regarding the gospel and non-Christian religions.

The apostle Paul warned the Christians at Corinth not to participate in the worship of idols. He said that "the sacrifices of pagans are offered to demons, not to God, and I do not want you to be participants with demons" (1 Corinthians 10:20).

The apostle Paul described the spiritual condition of the Ephesians before their conversion to Christ (Ephesians 2:1–3).

He said that they were dead in their transgressions and sins, they followed the ways of the world and of the ruler of the kingdom of the air (Satan), and they were objects of the wrath of God.

There is no place in the Bible where the subject of the gospel and other religions is more clearly treated than in the first chapter of Romans. Paul begins by describing the gospel as a message from God. It is a message revealed in the Holy Scriptures, centered in Jesus Christ the Son of God, and intended to be proclaimed to people everywhere, calling them to obey God by believing in Jesus Christ. This gospel is

> the power of God for the salvation of everyone who believes: first for the Jew, then for the Gentile. For in the gospel a righteousness from God is revealed, a righteousness that is by faith from first to last, just as it is written [in the Old Testament]: "The righteous will live by faith." (Romans 1:16–17)

Messengers of the gospel must preach it everywhere, to people of all nations, races, tribes, and social classes. All who believe it become the children of God. God loves them and declares them "holy" in Christ.

The subject changes at verse 18 to the spiritual condition of those who do not believe in Jesus Christ but worship other gods. Romans 1:18–32 declares the following:

- The wrath of God is against them (verse 18).
- God reveals to them plainly that he exists and that he is powerful and eternal (verses 19–20).
- They see this, but they ignore it, leaving themselves without any excuse (verse 20).
- They suppress the revelation God gives about himself and choose to worship things that men make rather than the Creator, to whom all worship should be given (verses 21–23).

- They suffer the consequences of their decision to follow the sinful desires of their hearts (verses 24–25).
- God punishes those who worship other gods, and all the suffering and evil in the world are due to the rebellion of the human race against the true God and his rule over their lives (verses 26–32).

The apostle Paul places his finger on the deadly sickness of all other religions. In one way or another, they deny or neglect the true nature of God as he reveals himself. Some religions identify God with the world and with the inner forces of human nature. In other religions, God remains at a great distance, far removed from human beings. In either case, people do not submit to him or worship him as he desires.

We see people everywhere desiring to know God and at the same time running away from God. This is the essence of all other religions. They substitute other gods for the only true and living God. The apostle Paul says that they know that God exists, but they do not worship him or give him thanks for all his blessings. They exchange the glory of the eternal God for images and worship them instead.

TRUTH AND BEAUTY IN OTHER RELIGIONS

It is sometimes said that truth, even the truth of salvation, can be found in other religions. People point to the beautiful things written by Hindu and Muslim mystics, and they ask, Are there not beautiful truths in other religions? Is it not possible that people who are deeply sincere can be saved by other religions as well as by the Christian gospel?

Nobody can deny that many followers of other religions are deeply sincere. Some of their poems and songs sound on the surface like Christian hymns and prayers. We hear them and we ask, Who is the god to whom they pray and offer their worship? Is this the kind of praise and worship that Jesus said his Father seeks (John 4:23)?

The teachings of the Bible are the only reliable basis on which to answer these questions. We should not speculate on matters of such great importance. We should listen to what God himself has revealed in the Bible about his work among those who do not know or believe the gospel.

First, the Bible teaches that every human being has a mysterious knowledge of God. It never becomes a true and saving knowledge because it is suppressed by falsehoods and wickedness. There is, nevertheless, an element of true religious knowledge in the ignorance of unbelievers and among all their false ideas (Romans 1:18–20).

Second, all human beings have a hunger for God that they seek to satisfy in one way or another. God created all of us in his image, which means that he put in us the need and capacity to know God and to have fellowship with him (Genesis 1:26–27). John Calvin spoke about "the seed of religion" that God put in every human heart. By itself, that seed never grows into true faith in the one true God.

The Fall occurred, and it corrupted everything (Genesis 3). The relationship with God that Adam and Eve had enjoyed was broken. The human race moved further and further away from God from that point on. People made religions of their own choosing instead of worshipping the God who created them. This is the reason for the multitude of religions in the world.

Third, the Bible teaches that God has not left himself without a witness to all people of the world (Acts 14:17). God has spoken and continues to speak to all people in various ways. There are elements of truth everywhere for this reason.

HOW HAS GOD SPOKEN?

First, the Word of God is heard in old traditions handed down from one generation to another from the beginning of history. The human race has not entirely forgotten truths contained in old traditions about God the Creator and about paradise and how it was lost. Old traditions of this kind are found around the world.

Second, God also speaks in nature. Everything we see around us declares the glory of God and displays his creative power (Psalm 19:1). Evidences of the existence, power, and glory of God surround every human being.

Third, God reveals his moral justice through the experiences of life. Every human being has a conscience, and it gives some sense of right and wrong (Romans 2:15). It also gives people a sense that in some way they are accountable to a supreme being who rewards and punishes people's actions.

We can see throughout history that God punishes evil and rewards good. The Hindu doctrine of *karma* reflects this. *Karma* means the eternal law of rewards and punishments. Even those who worship other gods perceive the justice and power of God.

God also has spoken to the world through the preaching of prophets, apostles, and missionaries. Christians have been going everywhere and proclaiming the Word of God since the Day of Pentecost.

God has revealed himself most clearly through the written Word, the Bible. The Bible has traveled around the world for many centuries. Jews translated the Old Testament into Greek, and its teachings about the Creator, the Fall, and the moral law of God became widely known before the birth of Christ. The early apostles used the Old Testament in Greek in their mission work.

Christians have translated the Bible into many languages and have distributed it around the world. Elements of the gospel of grace have gone far beyond the church. They have affected religions and cultures that do not carry the name "Christian" at all.

These elements of truth have not remained clear and pure

enough to offer salvation to followers of other religions. Although pieces of truth have become part of other religions, they have been polluted to such a degree that they no longer communicate the Christian gospel so that people can be saved by them.

Therefore, missions remain necessary. Followers of other religions must not be left with only small pieces of truth. Christians must go and tell them the full gospel of Jesus Christ and invite them to leave their old gods and worship the one true God alone.

TELLING THE STORY OF JESUS

Christians who study books written by poets and mystics of other faiths are often impressed by their beautiful language. Likewise, Christians who dialogue with followers of other religions are often impressed by their sincerity and dedication to their faith.

Are they nearer to God and to the gospel than Christians have supposed? On a personal level, can we distinguish true worshipers of God from those who worship something entirely different?

There is a way to find the answer. *Tell them the story of Jesus!* Tell them that the God who created the world and who made us all in his image still loves the world. He sent his Son into the world to pay for our sins and reconcile us to himself. Tell them the story of the cross and the resurrection. Urge them to repent from their sins and believe in Jesus as their Savior and Lord. Tell them that all who repent and trust in Jesus become the children of God and inherit eternal life. Invite them to become disciples of Jesus Christ and obey him in all areas of their lives.

If someone responds by saying, "This is who I always believed God to be! I have been waiting for years to hear the story as you told it! Tell me more!" you can be sure in this case that such a person had a beginning of true faith in God long before you told the story of Jesus.

People of this nature are very rare. You probably will not find one in your lifetime, even though it is popular to imagine that bright rays of light can be found in all religions. Such ideas are contradicted by the facts, however. The powers of darkness are strong, and the deceptions of Satan are great.

What you will find when you speak to most people about Jesus is the same as what the apostle Paul found among those who rejected the gospel in his day: "The god of this age has blinded the minds of unbelievers, so that they cannot see the light of the gospel of the glory of Christ, who is the image of God" (2 Corinthians 4:4).

God alone can make the light shine in their hearts and give them the true knowledge of the glory of God as it shines in the face of Jesus Christ. God does this through the preaching of the gospel (2 Corinthians 4:5–6).

REVIEW QUESTIONS

1. Give five characteristics of the religion of the covenant as taught in the Old Testament.

2. Why is it important to know what the Old Testament said about other religions?

3. What does 1 Corinthians 10:20 say about sacrifices to other gods?

4. How do you explain elements of truth that are found throughout the world?

5. Explain as fully as you can the teaching of Romans 1 concerning (a) the gospel and (b) other religions.

Discussion Questions

1. What value can you see in dialogue between followers of different religions, and what mistakes should you avoid?

2. Some people are called pluralists because they regard all religions as equally true; others are considered inclusivists because they believe that somehow Jesus saves the sincere followers of all religions; and some are exclusivists, who insist that knowing and believing in Jesus is the only way to be saved. Which position do you take, and why?

3. Suggestion: Divide into small groups and ask one person in each group to present the gospel to the group as though he were explaining it to followers of another religion.

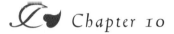 Chapter 10

The Uniqueness and Finality of Jesus Christ

Robert E. Speer was a mission leader in the early decades of the twentieth century. In 1932 and 1933, Speer delivered a series of lectures on missions to two of the leading seminaries in North America. The first was Princeton Theological Seminary, which was Presbyterian. The second was Southern Baptist Theological Seminary, which was the largest of the Baptist seminaries at that time. Speer said the following in his opening address:

> We are facing, today, in the Christian Church at home and in the missionary enterprise abroad, the fundamental questions of the meaning and value of Christ and of the nature of Christianity. Is Christ unique, final, absolute, and universal? Is He the world's only Savior and Redeemer? Is He God and the only Son of God? Or was He only one of us and no more, a fellow-seeker after truth and life, perhaps an example still ahead of us, or perhaps not an example of any authority at all, but only a Galilean peasant hemmed in by many limitations which we have transcended, or, at the most, a great religious genius, worthy to walk with or lead the company of Buddha, Zoroaster, Mohammed, Lao-tse, and now as some say, Mahatma Gandhi?

As to the nature of Christianity, is it the final and absolute religion, or is it only one of the family of sister religions, each worked out by and adapted to the ethnic character which produced it, and has it any mission to conquer the whole world, or should it seek adjustment and synthesis with other religions, recognizing its essential unity with them in their fundamental conceptions and ideals, and come to terms also with all non-Christian philosophies? These are not mere academic and theoretical questions. They are the central issues that the Christian faith is meeting today in the East and West alike. (*The Finality of Jesus Christ*, 12)

How contemporary Robert Speer's words sound! Though he spoke them many years ago, they address the most important questions facing the Christian church and missions today: *What do we mean by the uniqueness and finality of Jesus Christ, and do we have any right to make such claims and proclaim them to the world?*

FROM THE TIME OF THE BIBLE TO THE TWENTIETH CENTURY

The Bible teaches enormous truths about the person and work of Jesus Christ. The Bible says that he is the Way, the Truth, and the Life. He is the only Mediator between God and mankind. He is the resurrection and the life. He is the only one who can teach us to know God the Father.

The church has affirmed the central place of Jesus Christ throughout the centuries. The early church gave much attention to setting forth and explaining Christ's *divinity*. The Protestant Reformers affirmed that Christ is the complete and only *Savior*. In the *Heidelberg Catechism*, for example, which is one of the basic confessions produced by the Reformed churches, they declared that "salvation cannot be found in anyone else; it is futile to look for any salvation elsewhere" (Question and Answer 29).

Protestant leaders emphasized the doctrines of salvation by grace alone through faith in Christ and of the authority of the Bible. The uniqueness of Christ as the only Savior of the world was not an issue in their time.

Doubts regarding the uniqueness of Christ began to arise in the twentieth century. Some people suggested that God might reveal himself through other religions as well as through Christ and the Bible. Some scholars placed Christ on the same level as saviors and teachers in other faiths.

Many Christians became concerned that this trend would compromise the integrity of the gospel. One organization, the Reformed Ecumenical Council (R.E.C.), composed of Reformed and Presbyterian churches throughout the world, decided to make a special study of the issue and then published a report titled *The Unique Person and Work of Christ*. Its statement can serve as a testimony and a guide for all Christians. I helped to draft the report, and I draw from parts of it in the discussion that follows.

1. Christ is unique as the only Savior and Reconciler.

The story of the Bible can be summarized by the themes of creation, fall, redemption, and restoration. God created the world good, but it became separated from him and hostile to him through sin. Rather than turn away, God chose to redeem the world and restore it to himself through his Son, Jesus Christ. The single act of divine intervention for the purpose of reconciling a lost world to himself was the coming of Jesus Christ into the world.

Other religions have sought to establish grounds for reconciliation. The Christian gospel, however, witnesses to the one and only sure basis of reconciliation: the incarnation, atonement, and resurrection of Jesus Christ. All people on earth have a sense of being lost. All seek salvation in some way. Christianity insists that the only true way is Christ.

2.   Christ is unique as the Peacemaker between races, tribes, and peoples.

Reconciliation between God and redeemed sinners in Christ offers a new opportunity for reconciliation to occur between human beings. The Bible speaks in Ephesians 2:13–16 of the Body of Christ, the church, as a new humanity, a unified humanity that replaces the old division between Jew and Gentile. The way to reconciliation is opened to all races, tribes, and nationalities through the cross of Christ. The church should demonstrate this reconciliation.

This is very important to missions. We build the most interracial and multicultural institution in the world through missionary activity. The church is a wonderful testimony to the reconciling grace of God in Christ in many places, but the church has not overcome racial, tribal, and national prejudices and hostilities in other places.

The church ought to be a sign of how humanity can live together in all its diversity in peace in Christ. The blood of Christ and citizenship in his kingdom are powerful forces for unity. They should make us overcome all racial, cultural, and national differences among believers.

"Christ the unifier" needs to become a vital part of our missionary message. Christ shed his blood for the peoples of the world. The blood he shed was human blood, which Christ shared with all the peoples of the world by his incarnation.

Our primary identity is no longer our biological family, our race, tribe, or nationality when we are born again in Christ. Our primary identity is our place in the family of God. Believers are brothers and sisters in Christ. We need to proclaim this and demonstrate it. This belongs to our mission.

3.   Christ is unique as the teacher and manifestation of truth and righteousness.

There is a close link in Christ between truth and righteousness. *Truth* means knowing something as it really is. *Righteousness* refers to right moral behavior. The problem for human beings is that by nature we are not righteous. We are sinners.

That is where Jesus provides the solution. We are *made righteous* through Christ's atonement. Christ bore the punishment for our sin. It was God's divine plan of redemption that Jesus' perfect righteousness be credited to all who believe in him. Second Corinthians 5:21 says, "God made him who had no sin to be sin for us, so that in him we might become the righteousness of God."

The R.E.C. report states it this way:

> By linking righteousness and truth in the unique person of Christ, we are implying that only in this relationship that God initiated can we know truth. There is no perception of truth outside of our relationship with Christ, the one appointed to be our mediator and redeemer. (17)

Thomas asks Jesus, "Lord, we don't know where you are going, so how can we know the way?" (John 14:5–6). Jesus answers, "I am the way and the truth and the life. No one comes to the Father except through me." The three key words ("way," "truth," "life") have a small word in front of them in the Greek language in which the New Testament was written. This small word indicates that Christ *alone* can be called by these key words.

The message is clear: Jesus Christ is related uniquely to God the Father. No one comes to the Father except through Jesus. He is the way of *life,* not death. He is *truth in all that he says and does.* Satan offers lies and death. Jesus offers truth and life. Trusting him leads to life and to God.

Billions of people struggle to find out where they came from, where they are going, and why they are here in this world. The gospel of Jesus Christ offers true answers to these questions. It is the glory of missions to make this gospel known!

4. Christ is unique as the only Victor over Satan and sin.

Jesus Christ is unique not merely in the sense that every individual being is unique. He is unique because he is the Son of God. He was sent by the Father into this world on a mission: to reclaim the world from Satan. Every miracle Jesus performed brought the same message: The one who will crush the head of the Serpent has come into the world.

Miracles of healing, feeding the hungry, and raising the dead were all signals of Christ's victory over the power of Satan. Wherever Satan reigns there is sickness, hunger, and death, but where the kingdom of Jesus Christ is established, people are set free from the bondage of sin and the crushing control of Satan.

Jesus summed up his ministry in these words before his final sacrifice on the cross: "I will drive out demons and heal people today and tomorrow, and on the third day I will reach my goal" (Luke 13:32). Nobody else in all of history so deliberately and completely overcame Satan's power over human life. Christ reached his final goal when he broke Satan's control forever by rising victoriously from the grave. Now there is a bridge to God. The bridge is crossed by faith in Christ. No other religion offers this bridge. We point people to the bridge in missions!

5. Christ is unique as the only One who offers resurrection and eternal life.

All human beings want to be free from pain and suffering, from the feelings of guilt and shame, and from the weaknesses that afflict us. Everyone hopes that after death, conditions will be better. Religions try to satisfy these desires in different ways.

Only the Christian gospel offers unique answers. All the answers of the gospel have to do with Jesus Christ, and they really satisfy our deepest desires.

Again we see the importance of having a true, biblical worldview. A secular worldview has no place for God or the life to come. It offers no purpose for living beyond personal pleasure and satisfaction. Secularism teaches people to live for themselves and for the moment. Secularists assume that this is the only world there is and that death is the end of everything.

The gospel, on the other hand, provides a completely different worldview. God is at the center of life. The chief goal of human existence is to know God, enjoy his fellowship, and worship him forever. Jesus Christ gives hope of life beyond the grave and a place in heaven with him.

Once a person accepts the Christian worldview, his beliefs and perspective on life change radically. Life has purpose and value. He can endure even suffering because a better life lies ahead. Christ assures believers, "I am the resurrection and the life. He who believes in me will live, even though he dies" (John 11:25).

At the beginning of this chapter, we raised the question, Is Jesus really the only hope of the world? In truth, he is. There is finally only Jesus, and missions must go wherever this Jesus is not known and believed.

REVIEW QUESTIONS

1. State briefly the five unique aspects of Jesus.

2. Explain how reconciliation between peoples fits in the gospel.

3. How does a secular worldview differ from a biblical worldview?

DISCUSSION QUESTIONS

1. Why has the uniqueness of Christ become a major issue?

2. What will happen to missions if this truth is compromised?

3. How would you tell a Hindu or Buddhist about hope in Christ?

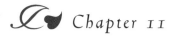 Chapter 11

Prayer and Missions

Samuel M. Zwemer was known in his time as the "apostle to Islam." He said that prayer and missions are so united that it is impossible to think of one without the other.

Andrew Murray was a mission leader in South Africa a century ago. He wrote a book entitled *Key to the Missionary Problem.* Murray identified the problem as a lack of passion toward Christ and toward lost people and the absence of prayer for the power of the Holy Spirit. Murray said that passionate love toward Christ produces a holy passion in believers like the passion Christ had that people be saved.

What produces such passion? The answer Murray gave was "Prayer!" Prayer like that at Pentecost—intense, united, continual. *When prayer for the power of God to do the work of God becomes the petition of every Christian, all the problems in missions will be solved.*

Frank Laubach was a missionary to the Philippines for twenty-five years. He taught illiterate people how to read, especially how to read the Bible. His motto was "Each one teach one." It is said that Laubach taught more illiterate people to read than any other man who ever lived. What motivated Laubach to extend his work throughout Asia, Africa, and South America? Laubach was a man of intense prayer.

Laubach made it a habit to spend hours every night wherever he was in private prayer for the poor, the lost, and the il literate. He would go off to a field or a garden, or lock himself in a bathroom, in order to be alone with God in prayer. He explained it this way:

> We shall be useful spiritually, only if we have a secret place to which we can run frequently for prayer. There we shall be recharged like a battery that has run down; and there we shall receive fresh instructions from our Lord. (*You Are My Friends*, 84)

There is a revival of prayer today among Christians around the world. This revival began in Latin America and South Korea. "Houses of prayer" are centers of Christian witness and growth in places like India. Prayer revivals lead to an increase in evangelism and missions, with few exceptions. As Samuel Zwemer said, *Prayer and missions are inseparable.*

PRAYER AND MISSIONS IN THE BIBLE

Many of the Old Testament psalms are prayers to God. A familiar petition is that the nations beyond Israel will learn to know the one true God and worship him alone. Psalm 67:1–3 is an example of this.

> May God be gracious to us and bless us
>   and make his face shine upon us,
> that your ways may be known on earth,
>   your salvation among all nations.
> May the peoples praise you, O God;
>   may all the peoples praise you.

We should not be surprised to find prayers for the nations within the book of Psalms. Psalm 2:8 says that the Father declared to the Son, "Ask of me, and I will make the nations your inheritance, the ends of the earth your possession."

Consider the petitions of the Lord's Prayer (Matthew 6:9–10).

> Hallowed be your name,
> your kingdom come,
> your will be done
> > on earth as it is in heaven.

No prayer is more missionary than this prayer. These petitions *require* missions and evangelism. The person who sincerely prays the Lord's Prayer hungers to see God praised and worshipped everywhere on earth. Jesus made prayer our most powerful weapon against the kingdom of Satan. By giving us this prayer, Jesus assures us that the gospel will triumph in the end.

Jesus said to his disciples, "The harvest is plentiful but the workers are few. Ask the Lord of the harvest, therefore, to send out workers into his harvest field" (Matthew 9:37–38). Jesus made it clear that the calling and sending of missionaries is primarily the work of God, for he is the "Lord of the harvest." Our primary task is to *pray* that he will call and send people of his choosing. We are assured that if we pray, he *will* send people.

The apostle Paul wrote more about the prayers he offered continually for believers, workers, and missionaries, than about anything else he did. Paul obviously considered prayer a matter of highest priority. Praying *is* missionary activity for Paul.

Ephesians 6:10–20 deals with the subject of spiritual warfare. Paul describes in detail the parts of the "armor of God" that Christians need to put on if they are to take their stand against the schemes of the Devil. The climax of Paul's instructions, after all the other parts of the armor have been identified, is this: "And pray in the Spirit on all occasions with all kinds of prayers and requests. With this in mind, be alert and always keep on praying for all the saints" (verse 18). Paul adds,

> Pray also for me, that whenever I open my mouth,
> words may be given me so that I will fearlessly make
> known the mystery of the gospel, for which I am an am-
> bassador in chains. Pray that I may declare it fearlessly,
> as I should. (verses 19–20)

Prayer is our most powerful weapon against Satan's attacks.
Prayer is the "secret weapon" of believers that the enemy cannot overcome. Paul acknowledged that he saw trouble ap-
proaching in Romans 15:30–33. He asked the believers at
Rome to "join me in my struggle by praying to God for me"
(verse 30). He wanted them to be his companions in spiritual
warfare ("join me in my struggle") as he traveled on a difficult
mission.

Much later, Paul was in a prison cell in Rome. He asked the
Colossians to pray that God would open a door, not for his re-
lease from prison, but a door for the gospel and for clarity in
proclaiming it. He said,

> Pray for us, too, that God may open a door for our mes-
> sage, so that we may proclaim the mystery of Christ, for
> which I am in chains. Pray that I may proclaim it
> clearly, as I should. (Colossians 4:3–4)

Second Thessalonians 3:1–2 is a summary of the request
Paul made repeatedly regarding prayer for missions.

> Finally, brothers, pray for us that the message of the
> Lord may spread rapidly and be honored, just as it was
> with you. And pray that we may be delivered from
> wicked and evil men, for not everyone has faith.

Why pray for missionaries? Paul gave the reasons. Missionaries need our prayers because they are people with normal
human needs, weaknesses, and problems. They are also people
whom God uses, for God's mission strategy is always to reach

the lost with his Word through the servants whom he sends (Romans 10:14–15). Missionaries are the objects of Satan's special attack and opposition, because God uses them. Satan is their enemy, as he is the enemy of God, and he uses many methods to prevent the spread of the gospel. Satan treats missionaries as "invaders" of his territory, and he does not give up a centimeter of territory without a fight.

God enables missionaries to gain ground against Satan through prayer. He gives them power to speak the gospel with courage and clarity, and they see people repent and turn to Christ. God opens doors and removes barriers in response to prayer. God is glorified through prayer as his kingdom advances.

It is no wonder that Paul asked the churches to pray for him. Paul was strong in faith, gifted as a missionary, and effective in his work, yet no one sensed more deeply than Paul the need for prayer. Prayer was missionary action for Paul.

PRAY, AND LOOK FOR THINGS TO HAPPEN

The missionary impact of John Miller will be remembered for a long time in North America, East Africa, and other places. Miller had many gifts, and he served with much fruit as a pastor, teacher, evangelist, church planter, and mission leader. Most of all, John Miller was mighty in prayer. He would pray anywhere, at any time, with anyone, and for anyone.

Miller urged students to become more serious about prayer when he taught at Westminster Theological Seminary in Philadelphia. Miller said to the students, "God knows you so well. He loves you and he wants to help you. He can give you more power, he can give you more fruit of the Spirit, and he can cleanse and use you beyond what you imagine." In one of his lectures, Miller said to the students,

> I'm asking you to rethink prayer . . . and to see in pray
> ing God's commitment to you as a Father listening to

his child. On the basis of that, be more daring when you pray. Be more definite, and more direct. Let me give you a short example. In one of my classes I asked my students to write on a piece of paper the names of five people they wanted to see converted to Christ. I asked them to commit themselves to pray daily for these five people, and for the convicting power of the Holy Spirit to come into their lives and turn them to Christ.

One student did it wrong. The first name he wrote was the name of a famous entertainer. "I didn't mean that kind of person," I said. "I want you to write names of people you know and can witness to yourself."

But what happened? Two weeks later the famous entertainer was converted! This taught me a lesson. God hears prayer, and God has his own ways of answering. So pray specifically, for specific people, even people whom you cannot speak to personally. And then look for things to happen. ("Prayer and Evangelism," 49)

Miller said we must be willing to look like fools both in prayer and in evangelism. Many Christians do not witness because they are afraid of looking like fools if people reject what they say. Likewise, they do not pray for specific people because they think they will feel foolish when nothing appears to happen. We need a fresh anointing of spiritual boldness to be specific in both praying and evangelizing. Only then will we learn what a sovereign and loving God may do.

PRAYING FOR PERSECUTED CHRISTIANS

The persecution of Christians is increasing in many parts of the world. Christians are the objects of discrimination in some places. In other places, they are arrested, tortured, and killed, their houses and churches burned, and their careers ruined. Christian children are taken from their parents. Church leaders, missionaries, and evangelists are usually the special objects of persecution.

We must recognize that those who confess faith in Christ in places where Christians are a minority and opposition to Christianity is strong often pay a high price. We should pray for them constantly. We must ask ourselves whether we are willing to serve God to the point of suffering.

In churches and classrooms, we speak of the "10/40 Window," the areas of the globe between the latitudes of 10 degrees and 40 degrees north of the equator from West Africa to Japan. These are the regions that are the least evangelized and have relatively few churches. A high percentage are poor. These regions are also the centers of Hinduism, Buddhism, and Islam. They represent the core of the kingdom of Satan.

We foresee the sacrifices of those who are Christ's witnesses in these lands. I conclude this chapter, therefore, with a quotation from Samuel M. Zwemer. Zwemer spent a lifetime knocking on closed doors in the Muslim Middle East, and he learned firsthand the importance of prayer for missions.

> Our first duty always and everywhere is to pray. If we do that, all other duties become easier. Unless we know the power of prayer, no great task is feasible. It is far easier to give of our substance to the missionary cause, or to go in person, than it is to pray truly for the Kingdom. In the light of eternity, it is astonishing how much time we spend in organizing or making big appeals, when the real work of missions must be accomplished on our knees. The present situation at home and abroad is first of all a summons to prayer. There never were so many open doors, nor so many doors that are closing! Never such response to the Gospel and never such bitter and determined opposition. In many lands the conditions are such that we have no other means to

enter them *than on our knees in prayer.* (*Thinking Missions with Christ*, 56–57)

REVIEW QUESTIONS

1. What should we remember about Zwemer, Murray, and Laubach?

2. Explain why the Lord's Prayer is a missionary prayer.

3. What specific things did Paul ask churches to pray for?

DISCUSSION QUESTIONS

1. Why is it hard to pray regularly for missions?

2. In what ways are we persecuted and how do we hold up?

3. Take John Miller's assignment and see what happens.

 PART 3

Issues in Missions

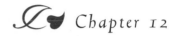 Chapter 12

Ministries of Prayer, Healing, and Exorcism

Jesus commissioned the disciples to go through the towns and villages of Israel, healing the sick, casting out demons, and preaching the gospel of the kingdom of heaven (Matthew 10). This was a declaration of war against the kingdom of Satan.

Jesus tied together the ministries of healing, exorcism, and preaching the gospel. The disciples understood this, and, from the beginning, prayers for healing the sick became part of the work of the Christian community. In churches whose leaders did not have miraculous gifts of healing, there was a ministry of prayer for healing (James 5:14).

Healings and exorcisms were not as prominent in the apostles' ministry as they were in Jesus' ministry. Signs and wonders occurred, but they were not central to the apostles' mission. Paul described his apostolic mission in Romans 15:18–20 by saying that signs and miracles *accompanied* his ministry and were a powerful *witness* to the truth of what he preached. His emphasis, however, was not on the signs and miracles but on the preaching of the gospel.

WHAT ABOUT MIRACLES TODAY?

Do miracles play a part in mission work today? How should missionaries deal with people who appear to be demonized? When we pray for the sick and troubled, do we pray in a way that shows we believe God is almighty and answers prayer for healing?

One of the weakest points in Western missions may be the failure to deal adequately with questions relating to sickness, healing, and demon possession. This failure has opened the door to extreme positions on both sides of the issue. Some missionaries explain healing almost entirely in terms of medicine and psychology, while others expect one miracle after another to occur. Perhaps missionaries from non-Western countries will show a more biblical approach.

THREE OBSERVATIONS ABOUT
UNSEEN SPIRITS AND THEIR INFLUENCE

We begin the discussion by observing three things.

1. *Belief in unseen spirits and their influence on human lives is a powerful religious idea around the world.*

Science and education have not stamped out belief in spirits and ideas about an invisible world. Educated people, wealthy people, people high up in government, and famous people in sports, movies, and television believe in spirits and regularly consult mediums of various kinds. Many people consult horoscopes. They may laugh at what the Bible teaches about God and the supernatural events the Bible describes, but they take seriously all kinds of unbiblical theories about invisible spirits and how they affect human lives. Fortunetellers and astrologers enjoy a good business because people believe in these things.

2. The unseen world has probably been taken more seriously among missionaries than among most other Christian leaders.

For years missionaries reported that in the course of presenting the gospel they discovered what appeared to be cases of satanic activity. They also witnessed miraculous healings in answer to prayer. Missionaries told of times when they sensed they were being protected by angels. In some instances demons were cast out when Christians prayed.

People in both Western and non-Western societies are increasingly aware that modern science cannot explain everything. Western medicine does not offer the degree of healing that human beings need and seek. It is not surprising that books, movies, and television shows contain themes involving the supernatural. Even secular people talk about angels. It is obvious, therefore, that a secular worldview does not satisfy human needs and questions. People sense deep down in their hearts that an unseen world exists, and they want to be in touch with it.

3. Many of the fastest growing churches in the world are churches that emphasize prayer, practice healing, and regard "power encounters" in which the Devil is chased away as essential to Christian missions.

I am referring to Pentecostal churches of various kinds and their remarkable growth all over the world. My years in Latin America taught me to respect many Pentecostals for their zeal and passion for evangelism. I do not approve of the extremism of those who go beyond the teachings of Scripture in regard to healing and exorcism. I respect those who simply trust the mighty God of the Bible who sometimes does miracles when his children ask him.

Missions today needs a fresh awareness of three things: (1) *divine power,* which is available to the servants of God through the Holy Spirit; (2) the importance of *worldviews,* that is, the central beliefs and ideas that govern the thoughts and actions of individuals and communities; and, (3) the theology of the *kingdom,* that is, the lordship of Jesus Christ over all areas of life, which is a basic theme of Scripture.

None of us can give final answers to all the questions regarding miracles and missions, but I will try to shed some light on the issues.

MIRACLES AND THE THEOLOGY OF THE KINGDOM

Four truths related to the kingdom are important to keep in mind when we discuss Satan, demons, miracles, and exorcism.

1. Jesus Christ is the victorious King.

This truth is central in the New Testament. Jesus defeated Satan by his dying on the cross for sinners and rising from the grave. Satan is mortally wounded even while he continues to kick and bite. His destruction is guaranteed. Jesus proclaimed and demonstrated his victory over Satan and the kingdom of Satan in the Gospels every time he cast out demons, healed a sick person, or raised the dead.

2. Jesus Christ changes lives powerfully.

Paul's letters emphasize that the new life of believers, generated and maintained by the Holy Spirit, is a life characterized by *power.* It is power to change, power to overcome, power to serve, and power to witness.

3. Jesus Christ sets people free.

Jesus described his miracles of healing as setting free those whom Satan had bound and held captive. The bondage may be spiritual, moral, physical, or emotional. The captives may be individuals or whole tribes and communities. Christ sets captives free.

Captives of Satan dishonor God and bring ruin upon themselves. The gospel of the kingdom is all about Jesus setting captives free and empowering them to live to the glory of God.

4. Missions is, unavoidably, a power encounter.

From heaven Jesus said to Paul, "I am sending you to them to open their eyes and turn them from darkness to light, and *from the power of Satan to God,* so that they may receive forgiveness of sins and a place among those who are sanctified by faith in me" (Acts 26:17–18).

Satan has great power, and he does not give up one centimeter of territory without a fight. Paul knew that as a missionary he could be God's instrument in defeating Satan and setting people free by preaching repentance from idolatry and sin, conversion to Christ as Savior and Lord, and the prospect of radically changed lives through the power of the Holy Spirit (Acts 26:20).

WORLDVIEW AND THE "FLAW OF THE EXCLUDED MIDDLE"

Missions deals with the struggle between conflicting worldviews, each of them seeking to control the minds and hearts of people. Any flaw in our worldview will reduce the effectiveness of our missionary work.

"Worldview" means the answers people give to the most serious questions of life, such as questions about God, life after death, the value of prayer, and the reality of spirits. Worldviews determine the pattern of people's beliefs and values and eventually their behavior because worldviews function like the "control boxes" inside great machines.

The evangelical anthropologist Paul G. Hiebert understands the differences between the worldview of most Westerners and the worldview most commonly held among non-Westerners.

Hiebert explains that the universe of non-Western people generally has three levels. The top level has to do with heaven, where God is. The bottom level consists of the visible world that we can see, study, and explain scientifically. A middle zone between these two levels is invisible but very real. It is largely controlled by spirits, demons, ancestors, ghosts, magic, charms and fetishes, witches, mediums, sorcerers, and such powers.

The problem is what Hiebert calls the "excluded middle." Most Western missionaries have said very little about the middle level. They have not known how to deal with it because it has not fit the Western, scientific approach to reality in which they have been trained. They have not denied that the Bible speaks of angels and demons, signs and wonders, but they have pushed them all back into the distant past. They have interpreted Scripture in a way that has lost the significance of supernatural things for missions today.

DAMAGING RESULTS IN MISSIONS

One damaging result of this has been the neglect of the Bible's teaching that missions is spiritual warfare against Satan, "the god of this age" (2 Corinthians 4:4). It is treated as a theory to talk about rather than a truth to be applied to specific situations in evangelism.

Prayer is another example. In Western churches, prayer is regarded as something all Christians should do because the Bible teaches it. Non-Western observers point out that something is missing in the Western way of praying. Many Christians in the West seem to lack the expectation that God can save, heal, change lives and circumstances, and set people free *now*.

Most Western-trained missionaries are not prepared to deal with those parts of reality associated with unseen spirits, demon possession, and the level of demonic activity found wherever the gospel is invading the territory of Satan. I was shocked by the evidences of demonic influence when I began my ministry in Sri Lanka. My training in seminary and in a well-known school of missions had not prepared me for what I encountered in Asia, and as a result I was largely ineffective for some time. I may have contributed to the growth of secularism among the people by the extent to which I avoided issues involving the invisible world of spirits.

Syncretism, uniting ideas and practices that ought to remain separate, is another consequence of the "excluded middle." It is common to find Christians who profess evangelical doctrines, yet also consult astrologers, contact mediums in times of crisis, and occasionally resort to using fetishes and occult rituals. Such people have not found satisfactory answers to their questions about the unseen world in Christian teaching. Consequently, their faith in Christ has not grown as it should, and they fall into the error of religious syncretism.

SOME PRACTICAL APPLICATIONS

I am thankful that missionaries are moving toward a better understanding of what it means to proclaim with power the gospel of King Jesus in a world in which satanic forces are at work. The current revival of prayer around the world is one sign of this. We need to take seriously everything the Bible teaches about Satan, demons, and spiritual warfare. However, we ought not to probe beyond what the Holy Spirit has revealed in the Bible. Interviewing demons is foolish and dangerous. Nothing they say can be trusted.

In spiritual ministry, we must avoid having others look at us as "shamans," persons with special powers to influence or manipulate the unseen world. If and when God uses us to defeat Satan and cast out evil spirits through prayer, make sure all the glory goes to God.

REVIEW QUESTIONS

1. What role did miracles play in the apostles' mission?

2. Explain "worldview" and its importance in missions.

3. What four things about the kingdom must we keep in mind?

4. Explain what Paul Hiebert means by the "excluded middle."

DISCUSSION QUESTIONS

1. What experiences have you had with miracles of healing?

2. How do you interpret what the Bible teaches about spirits?

3. How does your church or mission try to put a stop to syncretism?

4. If some Christian friends brought a demon-possessed person to you, what do you think you would do?

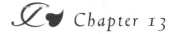 *Chapter 13*

Leadership Development for Church Growth

The Presbyterian Church in southern Mexico has over 1500 congregations, but only 350 ordained ministers. The seminary that serves these congregations produces only twenty-five to thirty-five graduates each year. As a result, many ministers serve between five and fifteen congregations. Because some of the congregations are at a great distance, the ministers do a great deal of hard traveling. More churches could be started, but there is already a shortage of ministers.

A seminary graduate in the city of Bogotá, Columbia told me he did not want to become an ordained minister because he did not want to be like a priest who travels from church to church. His denomination was so short of ministers that the few ministers they had were constantly traveling from one church to another baptizing and celebrating the Holy Communion. "They work just like the Catholic priests," he said. "They rush from place to place doing sacraments, but they do not get to know the local people, nor do they teach them by word and example."

Churches are growing so rapidly in some parts of the world that pastors cannot serve them effectively. There is the potential for more growth in other places, but there are not enough trained ministers to organize and lead new congregations.

Everything depends on the pastor in some churches, and lay members are not motivated or trained to do anything.

The apostles faced the challenge of raising up leaders for young churches in the early days of Christianity. They did not make churches depend on seminaries to give them leaders. Instead, the early missionaries trained local church leaders. Once trained, these leaders did not look to anyone from outside the congregation to provide weekly instruction, the spiritual care of a pastor, and direction in evangelism. They took care of their local congregations and saw them grow. The key to their success lay in training local leaders to carry on the ministry of the gospel in dependence on the Holy Spirit, the Scriptures, and the grace of God.

CHURCH GROWTH IN BALANCE

Donald A. McGavran will always be remembered as a mission leader who insisted that churches should *grow through evangelism.* McGavran spent most of his life in India, and he saw churches there surrounded by millions of lost people. The churches were doing little to evangelize them and plant churches among them. Christians were busy doing many good things, but none of those things had as their primary aim the winning of Hindus to faith in Jesus Christ and membership in the church of Christ.

McGavran knew from the Bible that Christ commanded his disciples to go into the world not simply to do good works, but to make disciples of all peoples. Christ wanted lost people found, won to him, and gathered into his church. What became known as the "Church Growth Movement" began from McGavran's teaching and writing.

Orlando Costas, a Latin American mission scholar, added important ideas to McGavran's emphasis on growth through evangelism. Costas insisted that to be healthy and balanced in a biblical sense, church growth should include not only growth in the number of people converted to Christ, but also spiritual growth shown by obedient and responsible discipleship.

Christians need to see the broader vision of the kingdom of Jesus Christ. Members of the church need to identify with their communities and transform them in terms of biblical values. Costas insisted that the growth of churches should lead to the growth of the lordship of Christ over all of life, over all human relationships, and over the natural environment and should inspire church members to continual growth. A key issue in missions is how to develop a sufficient number of effective leaders for the churches that are started. Churches seldom become stronger than the people who lead them.

PAUL, A TRAINER OF LEADERS

The apostle Paul is often regarded as a church planter, and rightly so. However, he not only started new churches, but he also spent a great deal of time and effort *training local leaders*.

Paul was an *initiator* in his role as an itinerant missionary. He introduced the gospel to people who had not heard it before, gathered believers, and organized churches. Paul knew that he would soon leave the new churches and go on to other places, but the churches would survive and grow if they had local leaders who worked hard, loved the people, and knew how to minister. Let us examine how Paul developed such leaders in Ephesus, a city where he planted a church.

The story of Paul's early ministry in the city of Ephesus begins in Acts 18:18. Paul arrived there with Priscilla and Aquila near the end of his second missionary journey. After he preached at the Jewish synagogue, the people asked him to stay longer. He declined, promising to return, but in the meantime he left Priscilla and Aquila, a dedicated Christian couple, to continue laying the foundation for his later return. The evangelist Apollos arrived at Ephesus during Paul's absence and added to the ministry by preaching the message of Jesus in the synagogue (Acts 18:24–26).

Acts 19 tells of Paul's return to Ephesus and the ministry he carried on in the city. Paul used persuasive arguments with the Jews in the synagogue and daily discussions with Gentiles in a public lecture hall. Miracles occurred and evil spirits were driven out (verses 1–12). People became afraid, and the name of Jesus was regarded with great respect (verse 17). New believers confessed their sins publicly (verse 18), sorcerers burned their occult books (verse 19), and the Word of God spread widely and with great power (verse 20). Men who made idols, however, saw their businesses in trouble because so many people were turning to Christ, and they started a riot (verses 23–41). Paul left the city when the riot stopped.

We read of Paul's "farewell" to the leaders of the church at Ephesus in Acts 20. Paul wanted them to remember clearly how he had planted and organized the church in their city, and to challenge them for the last time to carry out their responsibilities faithfully as leaders of God's people.

Paul began his farewell by reviewing his initial efforts at evangelism and making disciples: He visited people from house to house, developing deep and loving friendships with them. He preached in public and in private. He taught everything they needed to know about Christ and the gospel. He condemned false teaching and suffered persecution. He did manual work to support himself financially. He shed many tears when he and his message were rejected. His life and ministry were like an open book for all to see and read. He had no secrets. The theme of his life was "To live is Christ." His goal was "testifying to the gospel of God's grace" (verse 24).

Paul not only won converts in the process of this ministry; he also developed local leaders whom he called "elders" and "pastors." By the time he left, Paul had prepared these men to assume responsibility for maintaining the spiritual direction of the young Christian church without a continued dependence on him or anyone else. That was the key to Paul's success as a missionary and a church planter.

QUALITIES OF SPIRITUAL LEADERS

Paul found men at Ephesus who possessed the potential for leadership, and he trained them to the point that he could leave the church in their hands. Some of them were Jews who already knew the Hebrew Bible and its teachings. Others were Gentiles who came from pagan backgrounds. They had become mature in the faith under Paul's leadership. They also had grown in their understanding of the nature and function of the church, had gained experience in managing the affairs of the church, and had grown in confidence that the Lord could and would use them as leaders.

Spiritual leaders are people of prayer exercising the gifts of the Holy Spirit. Their special qualities are these:

- *Vision:* Leaders have spiritual "eyes" that let them see what God can do through the church and its ministry.
- *Tenacity:* Leaders can be counted on to keep on doing the work of the Lord despite difficulty and opposition.
- *Integrity:* Leaders can be trusted morally with money and with the care of people's souls.
- *Excellence:* Leaders want the church to function well in order to please God and serve people's needs.
- *Servanthood:* Leaders do not work for honor and power, but for the welfare of others and the glory of God.

THE TASKS OF CHURCH PLANTERS

Church planters have many tasks, among which are the following:

- to pray that God will develop the qualities of true leaders among the believers;
- to recognize these qualities when they appear, and train and develop those which possess them;

- to teach the members what to expect and require from those who will become their spiritual leaders. They should evaluate the character of Christian leaders not by the standards of the world but by the Word of God.

Church planters must give special training to those who show that they have the spiritual gifts to become leaders. Church planters must pray with them often, work alongside them, patiently explain the goals of ministry, and show them how to serve. They must delegate more and more responsibility without delay to the people whom they have trained. If disappointments come and people fall away, church planters repeat the process until reliable leaders are in place.

The goal is a group of local leaders who (1) are *models* of the faith and virtues of Christ in their lives, families, and daily activities; (2) *manage* the affairs of the church according to the teachings of the Word of God and for the welfare of the members; and (3) *multiply* in others the qualities that make leaders.

CHANGING ROLES

Missionaries need to recognize that in the course of planting and developing churches their roles must change as local leaders mature and develop. They must do almost everything at the beginning. Serious problems develop, however, if church planters continue to work in the manner in which they worked at the beginning when they alone possessed the wisdom and ability to direct the affairs of the church.

Effective church planters, according to the New Testament, are those who produce churches that can be turned over to local, spiritual leaders in a reasonable time while the church planters move on to start churches in new fields. We pity churches started by missionaries who want to remain in control forever, because hostility and division are sure to appear.

In some cases, missionaries may feel that God wants them

to remain as pastors of the churches they started. The rule for developing local leaders holds true even then. Pastors need leaders beside them who share the spiritual direction of the church. This is the only remedy for churches in which pastors are expected to do everything and the congregations cannot grow beyond the ability of one pastor to manage. Biblical leaders develop other leaders who in turn produce still more leaders, with the result that churches grow and multiply.

REVIEW QUESTIONS

1. After reflecting on the story of Paul's mission work at Ephesus, what important lessons do you learn from it?

2. What are the five special qualities of church leaders?

3. What happens when missionaries fail to train local leaders?

4. What actions would you take to train leaders around you?

DISCUSSION QUESTIONS

1. Identify and discuss the tasks of church planters.

2. Discuss your experiences with churches in which the pastors have to do all the work, and suggest how pastors might solve the problem.

3. Describe how you see the connection between planting churches and developing local spiritual leaders.

4. How would you attempt to solve the problems described at the beginning of the chapter?

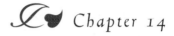 *Chapter 14*

The Challenge of the Cities

During the twentieth century, the world became urban. Only 13 percent of the world's population lived in cities when the century began. Half the world lives in cities as we enter a new century.

The migration of more than a billion people to the cities in the last two decades is the largest population movement in history. Biological growth, which is the number of births over deaths, adds greatly to this urban growth pattern.

Cities are the recognized centers of political power, economic activity, communication, scientific research, academic instruction, and moral and religious influence. Whatever happens in cities affects entire nations. The world goes in the direction that cities go.

Because of their size, influence, and needs, cities are the greatest challenge for Christian missions. The number of people who worship and serve God will greatly increase when Christian missions advance the kingdom of Christ in cities.

MEGACITIES OF TOMORROW

In 1950 only two cities, New York and London, had more than eight million inhabitants. There will be twenty-two by the end of the century. Thirty-three cities are expected to have more than eight million by the year 2015. Nineteen of these will be in Asia.

Analysts predict that by the year 2015 the populations of some of the largest cities of the world will be as follows:

Continent and Country	Millions*
ASIA	
Bangladesh	
Dhaka	19
China	
Beijing	19.4
Shanghai	15.1
Tianjin	10.4
Shenyang	9.4
Japan	
Tokyo	28.7
Osaka	11.6
Korea	
Seoul	13.1
Thailand	
Bangkok	13.9
India	
Mumbai	27.4
New Delhi	17.6
Calcutta	17.6
Hyderabad	10.4
Madras	8.4
Indonesia	
Jakarta	21.2
Pakistan	
Karachi	20.6
Lahore	10.6
Philippines	
Manila	14.7
AFRICA	
Nigeria	
Lagos	24.4
Zaire	
Kinshasa	13.9

Continent and Country	Millions*
EUROPE AND MIDDLE EAST	
Egypt	
Cairo	14.5
France	
Paris	9.6
Iran	
Teheran	14.6
Russia	
Moscow	9.2
Turkey	
Istanbul	12.3
NORTH AMERICA	
Mexico	
Mexico City	18.8
United States	
New York	17.6
Los Angeles	14.3
SOUTH AMERICA	
Argentina	
Buenos Aires	12.4
Brazil	
Sao Paulo	20.8
Rio de Janeiro	11.6
Peru	
Lima	12.1

* Much larger population figures are reported when they include both cities and the wider metropolitan areas around cities. The numbers above include cities only.

Keep in mind that every one of these millions of people is a human being made in the image of God. Each has many needs, and above all else each needs Jesus Christ and salvation through him. What a tremendous missionary challenge awaits us in the cities!

Causes of Rural-Urban Migration

The worldwide increase in population is an underlying cause of migration to the cities. People today generally live longer, infant mortality has decreased, and medicines keep people alive who, years ago, would have died. The need for more jobs comes with the increase in population. This forces millions to leave their traditional rural homes and move to cities in search of employment.

There are also other factors. Cities offer educational opportunities that are not available in small towns and villages. Cities offer hospitals and health centers for people with special medical needs. Young people, especially, are attracted to the cities for excitement, entertainment, and new opportunities. They often come to cities dreaming of riches and a better life, only to have their dreams destroyed by the hard realities of urban life.

Urban Poverty and Suffering

Some of the worst suffering is found among people that have recently arrived in cities. Peasants are seldom prepared for the difficulties they find in the city. They do not have the skills or training required for the jobs that are available. They do not have money to buy property or pay high rent. They are forced to live in squatter settlements, which are shacks built of pieces of wood, tin, and tar paper, usually located on the city borders.

In their early stages, squatter communities lack water, sewage, electricity, and regular streets. The residents are open to eviction and the sudden loss of their homes because the land does not belong to them. Those who are fortunate enough to find work must spend exhausting hours each day walking and traveling on public buses. Family life suffers as young and old work seven days a week at whatever jobs they can find.

Life for the poor is hard in cities. They are often the victims of crime and injustice. Nevertheless, large numbers of new people continue to arrive from the villages. They are drawn to the cities as though by invisible magnets. They have great hopes and dreams for the future despite the poverty and suffering they experience now. They firmly believe that if not the parents, certainly the children will enjoy better lives in the city.

OPENNESS TO THE GOSPEL

People who have recently relocated and are experiencing major changes in their lives generally are more open to the gospel than they were before. This has been true in my experience among people who have recently arrived in cities.

New people in the cities are open to new ideas, including ideas about God and religion. I believe that God is behind the migration of masses of people to the cities because he is creating new opportunities for spreading the gospel among unreached people coming from remote towns and villages. It is our task to take hold of the opportunity and carry out Christ's missionary command.

I worked with students in evangelizing and planting churches in squatter communities and other low-income areas during my years in Mexico City. First we tried other parts of the urban population. We found that the greatest openness to the gospel, however, was among people who had arrived in the city within the prior ten years.

We began dozens of "cells" and house churches by using the simplest and least costly methods: going door to door, witnessing personally to families in their homes, praying for the sick, and starting Bible studies. Many of these developed into well-established congregations. This led me to believe that the massive migration to the cities around the world may be, in the providence of God, a key to world evangelization. God is drawing people of every race, tribe, and language to places where they can be reached with the gospel through the growth of cities.

PRACTICAL ISSUES IN URBAN MISSIONS

1. Poverty

Between 30 and 50 percent of the population is poor in many cities, often *desperately* poor. Urban mission work, in most cases, demands that missionaries follow a broad strategy that proclaims the gospel of the saving love of God and demonstrates the same gospel in practical ways. Coping daily with social problems and economic differences is a very practical issue for urban missionaries.

2. Racial, Ethnic, and Cultural Diversity

In most countries, city populations are composed of people from many different backgrounds. They represent different tribes, castes, races, and social classes, and they speak different languages. This unavoidably affects mission strategy and church development.

3. Religious Pluralism

Most people follow one particular religion when they live in villages. City people, however, follow a variety of religious beliefs and practices. Urban missionaries may give major attention to one group, but they must be prepared to witness to others as well. They must also be prepared to respond to people who reject all religion and to others who regard all religions as equally true.

4. Anti-Urban Attitudes

Most mission work was traditionally done in rural areas. That made sense in the past because most people lived in rural communities. Now the biggest challenge is in the cities, but there we find a shortage of workers. Many missionaries are so disturbed by the noise and traffic in cities, the pollution, social problems, crime, and crowded housing, that they prefer working in rural areas. Unreached villages certainly need to hear the gospel. Yet, more attention must be given to the masses of unsaved and unchurched people in cities.

5. Financial Costs

A major practical issue for mission agencies is the higher financial costs of urban work. Housing for missionaries is more expensive in cities. A piece of land for a church building often costs little or nothing in the villages, and local believers can erect their own place of worship. Property in cities, though, is expensive, and building in the city means following building codes, dealing with labor unions, and paying higher wages. These and other factors tempt missionaries to avoid cities in favor of rural areas.

STEPS TOWARD ENGAGEMENT IN URBAN MISSIONS

I plead with all Christians who are concerned about doing the will of God and reaching lost people for Christ to consider the challenge of the growing cities of the world. A movement so large must have a divine purpose behind it and demands our response.

The question is not whether we prefer to live in cities. The question is whether we will go where workers are needed and where God wants us to go, just as it was for Jonah the prophet. Cities offer unique opportunities to reach great numbers of people with the gospel of Jesus Christ and extend his kingdom on earth.

I suggest certain steps for those of you who are beginning

to see what urban missions can accomplish in terms of the kingdom of God and are willing to explore what God may have in mind for you.

First and most important is your own spiritual development. Ministry in cities requires that you "put on the full armor of God" (Ephesians 6:11), not just once or occasionally, but daily. Therefore, stretch your spiritual horizons. Go beyond your individual spiritual development into ministries related to church and those in which you must pay a price in order to strengthen others.

Second, become involved in some kind of organized urban mission work. It will give you valuable experience and will test your gifts for ministry. Offer yourself as a "student" to an effective urban pastor, evangelist, or missionary. Observe carefully how the Lord uses his workers. Learn all you can about presenting the gospel to different kinds of people and meeting a variety of needs.

Third, read books and journals that deal with mission work in cities and learn all you can about different models of urban ministry. If possible, take a course in urban ministry at a Bible college or seminary. Some schools offer special programs in urban mission.

Fourth, investigate a particular city. Begin by studying a map of the city and identifying its different parts—commercial areas, industrial zones, and residential neighborhoods. Look closely at the areas that are growing in population and the kinds of people and cultures found there. Then choose one neighborhood and study its people—their religions, cultures, languages, and social conditions. Inquire about their spiritual, social, and material needs. Find out if there are vital churches in every language group. Think about ways to advance the kingdom of Christ in that particular neighborhood.

You will learn, by following these steps, to become an effective missionary and promote Christ's kingdom in the most strategic place in the world at this time—the cities.

REVIEW QUESTIONS

1. Explain why cities are so strategic for missions today.

2. Explain why millions of people are migrating to cities.

3. How should missionaries prepare themselves for mission work in cities?

DISCUSSION QUESTIONS

1. What factors should guide mission agencies in the division of workers between villages and cities?

2. What attracts you to cities, and what makes you want to avoid cities?

3. What needs to be done to change a neighborhood so that God is worshipped, his Word is obeyed, and human life is made healthy for all?

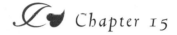 *Chapter 15*

Missions by Word and Deed

One beautiful Sunday morning, I watched hundreds of people arriving for worship in a West African town. "How was the church started?" I asked. "Who first brought the gospel here?"

The answer was this: "A woman missionary came to this town, and she was a nurse. Before she arrived, half of our children died before they reached the age of five. Then the missionary vaccinated our children. She taught the mothers how to keep their children healthy. She kept our babies from dying, and she taught us about God."

The church in that village was started through missions by word and deed.

I visited an elderly man in a slum where most of the people are Muslim. He, along with his four sons and their wives and children, had all become Christians. I asked the man what led him to leave Islam and put his faith in Jesus Christ.

He told me this story: "Christians came every week to our community and taught the Bible to a few Christians who lived here. They saw we were very poor, and they helped everyone. They helped the Christians, and they helped us Muslims. They did not charge anyone.

"For a long time I watched them to see what trick they intended to play on us. It made no sense to me that they helped Muslims and Christians in the same way, and without making us pay. There had to be a motive for the things they were doing.

"One day I asked them, 'Why are you doing this? What is your motive?' They answered me, 'We do it because God cares for everybody. God cares so much that he sent Jesus to save us by dying and paying for our sins.'

"God cares, and Jesus paid! That was a motive I had never heard before. I began to believe it was true. I started to pray to God in the name of Jesus Christ. My sons followed my example, and that is how we became Christians."

Missions by word and deed makes a powerful witness to Jesus Christ. It has opened up homes, towns, and nations to the gospel. It follows the example of Jesus himself, who "went through all the towns and villages, teaching in their synagogues, preaching the good news of the kingdom and healing every disease and sickness" (Matthew 9:35).

WHAT ABOUT THE "SOCIAL GOSPEL"?

Preaching the gospel ("word") and helping the poor and oppressed ("deed") were done together throughout most of Christian history. Early in the twentieth century, however, liberal theology entered many churches. Liberal theology denied basic teachings of the Bible, such as the virgin birth of Christ, the atonement, and the physical resurrection of Christ. Liberal theology promoted what was called the "Social Gospel" in missions.

People who were identified with the Social Gospel very often engaged in ministries among the poor, but there was a problem. They did not seek to convert people to faith in Christ as the Savior of lost sinners. They did not teach that the Bible was without error and the final authority in all matters of faith and practice. Their liberal theology took away the basic teachings of the gospel.

Many Christians who held to the authority of the Bible reacted to the Social Gospel. They believed in the necessity of personal conversion to Christ and the planting of churches, but they avoided social ministries that went beyond emergency relief. A wall was built between word and deed in missions, and the wall stood for fifty years.

Today, Christians in many parts of the world are working to break down the wall. They want to bring together word and deed so that they work together. We call this "holism" in missions. A "holistic" way to do missions recognizes that both the spiritual needs and the material needs of human beings are real and important. It is not biblical to ignore one or the other.

LIBERATION THEOLOGY

A movement known as "Liberation Theology" sprang up during the second half of the twentieth century in Latin America and spread over much of the world. Like the Social Gospel, Liberation Theology was mainly concerned about the poor and was weak in the areas of religious conversion and personal salvation.

Liberation Theology focused on oppression and the political and economic causes of poverty. The solution that it promoted contained strong elements of Marxism. Marxism was discredited by the end of the century, and Liberation theologians were left without the answers that they thought they had found. Liberation Theology tried to solve the problem of oppression and injustice, but the biblical gospel of the kingdom of God offers the only genuine solution.

We must look at the book of Genesis in order to understand the gospel of the kingdom. Genesis teaches that all human beings are made in the image of God (Genesis 1:26–27). Missions from the perspective of the kingdom takes this seriously. It takes the well-being of people seriously because it takes God seriously. God placed such high value on human beings that he sent his Son, Jesus Christ, to redeem them from captivity to sin, Satan, and hell. Christ took people so seriously that he sent his disciples into the whole world to preach the gospel of the kingdom.

Missions from the perspective of the kingdom regards any person or political or economic system that oppresses human beings as an enemy of Christ and his kingdom. To oppress a human being is to sin against God in whose image people are made.

It is no surprise that oppressors do not want the gospel to spread. Oppressors are the enemies of Christian missions because they know that the Word of God exposes their evil ways and threatens the kingdom of Satan that they represent. People whom Christ has freed from the bondage of sin and death do not submit easily to oppression imposed by men.

HOLISM IN MISSIONS: STRATEGY OF THE KINGDOM

Christ's command, "Go and make disciples," instructs us to proclaim the gospel of the kingdom throughout the world. The end of the world will not come until this command is fulfilled (Matthew 24:14).

This means

- calling people of all races, tribes, and nations to repent and follow Christ;
- caring for the poor, sick, and victims of oppression;
- planting and developing churches that preach the Word faithfully and proclaim the gospel to unsaved people nearby and far away;
- applying the lordship of Christ and authority of his Word to the lives of believers;
- promoting truth, righteousness, and reconciliation and opposing lies, evil, and conflict;
- caring for the whole creation—the water, soil, air, and trees—which God made for his glory and for the well-

being of the human race and which sinful people have treated badly.

The life of the kingdom is a life of truth, righteousness, mercy, and love. This life is proclaimed with words and demonstrated by deeds. The gospel of the kingdom embraces everything. It calls for the transformation of the heart and all of life. It governs how we live as individuals, families, and communities. It teaches us to show mercy to the poor, defend the oppressed, and seek reconciliation between hostile sides.

We realize how great and glorious the task of Christian missions is when we see the big picture of the gospel of the kingdom. The kingdom comes by missions into lives and places it had not come before. The righteousness of the kingdom is the hope of the world.

PRACTICAL ADVICE REGARDING MISSIONS BY WORD AND DEED

1. Christ must be lifted up in whatever we do and say.

Cups of cold water by the millions are needed, and they must always be given in the name of Christ. The errors of the Social Gospel ought not to be permitted to return. Good deeds alone are not enough. If missionaries do not speak of Christ and the saving grace of God to sinners, the gospel has no power to save.

2. Missionaries whose special gifts are preaching and teaching should not regard missionaries whose gifts are in other areas as "second class."

Let us eliminate all pride and arrogance among servants of the one Lord and Master, Jesus Christ. Some missionaries have more talents in agriculture, business, teaching languages, or translating than in preaching in front of a large group. The truth is that the Holy Spirit calls and uses many kinds of missionaries, each with special gifts.

3. Do everything possible to avoid long-term dependence on money and help from outside.

Dependency causes serious injury to churches and institutions when they ought to be standing on their own feet. Programs that missionaries begin should be placed in the hands of local Christians as quickly as possible. If local people cannot or will not take responsibility for them, in most cases the programs should be stopped.

4. The planting and development of churches that preach the Word and demonstrate compassion for the poor must be a goal of all mission programs.

Churches are lighthouses of the kingdom of God. There is no hope for the poor and lost without them.

5. Missionaries working among the poor should be careful not to appear to be taking advantage of their poverty in order to win them to the Christian religion.

Muslims and Hindus sometimes accuse Christians of trying to "buy" converts by offering help to them. We should not allow this accusation to divert us from helping the poor, but we should be careful not to give wrong ideas about the motives behind our deeds.

6. In cases of emergencies caused by war or natural disaster, "relief" work is appropriate. For long-term assistance, however, "development" is the best form of ministry to people in need.

Relief services do little to change long-term problems, and they often create a dependency on help from the outside. Development ministries on the other hand have as their goal enabling people who were poor to earn a respectable living on their own.

An old Chinese proverb illustrates the difference between relief and development. "If you give a hungry man a fish, you relieve his hunger for a day. If you teach him how to catch fish, you meet his needs for many days to come." Development protects the dignity of the poor and offers them the opportunity to rise up out of poverty and meet their own needs.

7. The work of missionaries does not end when groups of converts are won and churches are started.

The work moves on to equipping the young church by instructing members, training leaders, and helping to form ministries that carry the gospel to the entire community and eventually to distant places.

Missionaries set an example for new Christians to follow as they build the church. Missionaries maintain relationships and offer services to local Christians that testify to the unity and love that exist among believers. This unity and love reach across the differences of language, race, nationality, and culture. They proclaim to the world that despite surface differences, Christians truly are one. We all serve the same King, and his name is Jesus.

Review Questions

1. Explain what is meant by the Social Gospel and identify its principal errors.

2. What is the difference between the Social Gospel and Liberation Theology?

3. Describe the kingdom of Jesus Christ, and explain how holism promotes the kingdom.

4. Why do oppressors hate missions?

DISCUSSION QUESTIONS

1. When and where is "relief" the right thing to do, and how does relief differ from "development"?

2. Why is dependency harmful? Describe some situations in which long-term dependency may be unavoidable.

3. Give examples of mission work that testify to unity and love among Christians. How can we multiply these examples?

4. Describe four or more types of deed ministries that you have seen besides medical work. How effective are they in meeting human needs and drawing people to Jesus in your opinion? How would you change or improve them?

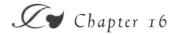 *Chapter 16*

Pastors, Evangelism, and Missions

Years ago, the missionary leader John R. Mott spoke about the key role that local pastors play in world missions.

> The secret of enabling the church to press forward in . the non-Christian world is one of leadership. The people do not go beyond their leaders in knowledge and zeal, nor surpass them in consecration and sacrifice. The Christian pastor . . . holds the divinely appointed office for inspiring and guiding the thought and activities of the church. By virtue of his position he can be a mighty force in the world's evangelization. (*The Pastor and Modern Missions*, 3)

Mott argued that in many cases the weak spot in missions is in the local churches and without the help of pastors the problem cannot be solved. Pastors set the direction that their congregations follow. Pastors are the teachers, models, and leaders. The fire of missions and evangelism will be kindled throughout the congregations whose pastors are on fire with a passion to reach the lost.

Mott believed that pastors who do not have a passion for missions cannot truly function as ministers of the gospel. They are spiritually weak. They are blind to the missionary message of the Bible. They do not understand that the primary work of the church is to make Christ known, obeyed, and loved throughout the world. They lack the fullness of the Spirit of Christ. Their congregations lack vision and power as a consequence, and missions suffers.

You do find very rare cases where a congregation evangelizes the lost while the pastor is lukewarm about missions. Missions stays alive in the congregation in such rare cases because of the strong influence of one or more lay members who are committed to missions. Usually, however, the pastor's missionary vision is the key to missionary vitality in the congregation. I will illustrate this.

How a Pastor Lost a Great Opportunity

Some years ago, my friend and missionary colleague Richard R. DeRidder was eating breakfast in his home in Colombo, Sri Lanka, when the telephone rang. The pastor of one of the larger churches in the city was on the line. He was a man about fifty-five years old, and he occupied a position of influence and leadership in his denomination. The church that he served was large and wealthy, but it did not engage in evangelism or support mission work.

The pastor sounded troubled. "Richard," he said, "there is a Buddhist monk at my door who says he wants to become a Christian. What do I do with him?" Richard suggested that the pastor take the Bible and explain to the monk that the God who made heaven and earth provides salvation for sinners by grace and through faith in Christ. "But, Richard," replied the pastor, "I am not good at that kind of thing. Can you come over here and take care of him?"

Richard went over to the pastor's house as quickly as he could. There sat the Buddhist monk dressed in his yellow robe. The monk told a fascinating story. He had studied the Bible in secret for several years. He had taken Bible correspondence courses, using the name and address of another person so that other monks would not learn what he was doing. Finally, he decided to become a Christian and went looking for a Christian minister.

The monk knew nothing about different churches or denominations, so he chose the biggest church on the main street of the city and asked to see the pastor. Unfortunately, it was a pastor who knew nothing about evangelism or how to present the basic truths of the gospel to a leader from another religion.

Thank God that Richard knew what to do. He spent the rest of the day with the monk, answering questions and explaining the truths of the Christian faith. By the time night came, the man was asking how soon he could be baptized.

The story illustrates the missing element in the thinking and ministry of many pastors. This pastor had led a large congregation for many years, but he had no vision for reaching lost people for Christ. He did not lead his members to evangelize, nor did they support mission work. It was not surprising, therefore, that the pastor failed when the opportunity came to lead a monk to faith in Christ. This could have been a great moment in his ministry, but he had to call someone else because he himself did not know how to evangelize.

A SAD DISCOVERY

I met George Peters at a conference on world evangelization held in Thailand some years ago. He taught Missions for many years at Dallas Theological Seminary. Peters made trips to Europe to speak to pastors when he retired from teaching. One gathering had over 350 European pastors. Peters asked the pastors how many had ever studied evangelism. Five pastors said that they had taken a course in the subject. Twenty had attended a one day workshop. The rest had never received any training at all in evangelism, nor did they know much about world missions. Their theology did not motivate them to preach Christ to the lost.

Peters asked himself if there was any connection between this lack of interest and training in evangelism and the major complaint throughout Europe that the churches were not growing, and he concluded that there was a very close connection. Most European churches and the schools used to train pastors did not join pastoral ministry together with evangelism and missions to a lost world.

WHEN PASTORS FAIL

A series of bad things happen when pastors fail to present Christ's claims to the unsaved. First, the gospel of divine, saving grace no longer shines from the pulpits. Then members see no need to spread the gospel. They become involved instead in activities that are not bad, but do not communicate the gospel in a clear way.

A major concern among some church members is *ecumenism,* or cooperation between churches. They talk about *dialogue* with people of other religions instead of evangelism. The *environment* is another concern, and many of them are more interested in saving trees, whales, and birds than in saving eternal human souls. The proclamation of salvation through faith in Christ is absent, and the conviction that lost people need to be converted and saved is gone.

Bill Hybels, pastor of the Willow Creek Community Church near Chicago, is correct when he says that *an evangelizing church is the hope of the world, and the renewal of the church in evangelism rests in the hands of its leaders.*

JESUS, THE PASTOR WITH A PASSION FOR SOULS

Who can teach us more about evangelism than Jesus? Who is a better leader than he? Jesus is called the Chief Pastor

(Shepherd) in 1 Peter 5:4. All the lesser leaders of the church serve under him. Hebrews 13:20 calls Jesus the Great Pastor (Shepherd), for he is the perfect model for us to follow. All of us who are called to be leaders of God's people must give account to Jesus as to how closely we come to him in heart, attitude, and conduct.

Look at Jesus and his ministry. He taught the disciples and reached out to the lost. He showed what true pastors should do by his teaching and example. He fed his sheep by teaching. He sought the lost by preaching from one place to the next. He showed that he loved the world by sending his disciples to the ends of the earth. Jesus demonstrated the heart of a pastor in every way. He was a pastor who, at great sacrifice to himself, even death, came to seek and to save the lost.

In the parable of the lost sheep, Jesus described the joy that he and his Father felt when lost sheep were brought home (Matthew 18:12–14; Luke 15:4–7). The heart of God is revealed in the picture of the shepherd carrying the sheep in his arms and bringing it back to the fold. Jesus is the perfect example of bringing sinners home to God and caring for them. This is the sacred office of pastors.

No other religion has a Pastor or Leader like Jesus, nor is there anything equal to the Christian pastor in other religions. Jesus showed how far he would go in order to save the lost by his suffering and death. He went to the cross in order to fulfill the saving purpose of his heavenly Father. The work of pastors and missionaries is one with that divine purpose.

PAUL AND TIMOTHY

Paul reminded the elders of the church at Ephesus that in his ministry among them he had not separated evangelism from pastoral ministry. He had evangelized, taught sound doctrine, organized the congregation, developed the members in faith and service to the poor, and trained the local leaders.

Paul expected these leaders to follow his example in the future (Acts 20:17–38).

Paul said to the young pastor Timothy that he should "do the work of an evangelist" (2 Timothy 4:5), and by so doing carry out all the duties of his ministry. What did Paul mean by this? Did he mean that Timothy had *two* jobs, first to be a pastor and second to be an evangelist? Not at all!

The Bible scholar William Hendriksen pointed out in his *New Testament Commentary on I–II Timothy and Titus,* that in the Greek text there is no definite article before the word *evangelist.* This means, says Hendriksen, that Paul did not intend to give Timothy a "second job." Paul intended to emphasize for Timothy *the evangelistic character of all pastoral duties.*

When Paul said, "Do the work of an evangelist," he was saying, Timothy, your pastoral work should be *evangelistic in character wherever you go and whatever you do. You are a pastor-evangelist, which means you are never a pastor without being an evangelist at the same time.* All pastors are called like Timothy to care for their congregations (Acts 20:28; 1 Peter 5:2–4), seek the lost (Matthew 18:12–14; Luke 15:3–7), and protect believers from false teachers (Acts 20:29–31).

PASTOR-EVANGELISTS TODAY

Pastor-evangelists fulfill their responsibilities as leaders in evangelism and missions in three ways:

(1) *by teaching and preaching* evangelism and missions from the Scriptures and showing the members how to pray for the spread of the gospel throughout the world;

(2) *by personal example* as pastors see and use the opportunities they have to tell the gospel to unbelievers in homes, hospitals, buses, and streets;

(3) *by organizing their congregations, including young people,* for evangelistic activities such as Bible studies in jails

and prisons, in homes, schools, and offices, and services to the poor by which they testify to the love and mercy of God by their words and deeds.

Charles L. Goodell says the following about the work of a pastor in an old book entitled *Pastor and Evangelist* (p. 110):

Lost people, like lost sheep, do not come home of themselves. They have to be sought. It is not enough to build your church and to stand in your pulpit and say, "Come." You have to go out and seek, if you would save.

When the passion for souls dies out, then all sense of the reality of religion perishes. It is when we see Him healing people that we have faith in the great physician. It is when we see the lost being saved that we believe in Christianity. And when the passion for the lost dies out in the pulpit, people will shiver around its cold ashes instead of warming their souls at the blaze of a light which was kindled in the heavens.

Let us get then a clear conception of what the pastor is. The pastoral function is nothing more nor less than to watch over the sheep and to bring those who are straying back into the fold. Is it not time to go back to the one business for which the Church of God was organized and inspired?

REVIEW QUESTIONS

1. Summarize what John R. Mott said about the role of pastors.

2. What happens when pastors do not promote evangelism?

3. What did Paul mean by "Do the work of an evangelist"?

4. How do pastor-evangelists fulfill their calling?

DISCUSSION QUESTIONS

1. When pastors ignore evangelism, who is most to blame, the pastors or the schools that trained them? Explain.

2. Imagine that Jesus examined what your congregation is doing in evangelism. What would he like, or not like?

3. Describe opportunities that come especially to pastors to tell unbelievers about Christ.

4. What does reading this chapter move you to pray for?

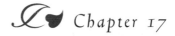 *Chapter 17*

Financial Support for Missions

How should missionaries and their work be supported financially? Like everyone else, missionaries need money to pay for food, housing, and other necessities. Missionaries who are married and have children have even greater financial needs.

Missionaries generally have more expenses than average people. Their work requires that they travel, and travel by bus, car, boat, airplane, or motorcycle costs money. They must buy their food and pay for lodging when they are away from home. Missionaries need money not only to sustain themselves but also for Bibles, literature, and other means they use to proclaim the gospel wherever they work.

TENTMAKERS

Missionaries sometimes can find local employment and support themselves by their own work. We call such missionaries "tentmakers." They follow the example of the apostle Paul who worked alongside Aquila and Priscilla as a tentmaker in Corinth (Acts 18:2–3).

There are advantages to being a "tentmaker." Daily employment in a school or business gives the missionary financial support and also personal contacts with local people. Contacts of this kind are valuable. Regular employment also gives missionaries identity in the community. They are "strangers"; but when they are employed, they enjoy the advantage of being identified with the school or other institution where they work.

"Tentmakers" also face certain problems. One problem is that their daily employment occupies much of their time and energy. A second problem is that their employers may prohibit them from engaging in religious activities of any kind.

"Tentmaking" is impossible in some countries because their governments do not allow foreigners to take employment. They may enter the country as "visitors," but they are not allowed to earn money. Missionaries have to depend on believers in other places to provide what they need if there are no local Christians to support them.

NEW TESTAMENT TEACHINGS ABOUT SUPPORTING MISSIONARIES

The New Testament contains many instructions about supporting the servants of the Lord. The apostle Paul wrote to the Corinthian Christians that "the Lord has commanded that those who preach the gospel should receive their living from the gospel" (1 Corinthians 9:14). This teaching was based on the laws of the Old Testament. God commanded that priests and Levites should be supported by the offerings of the people (Leviticus 7:28–36; Numbers 18:8–21).

Jesus sent his disciples to the "lost sheep of Israel" and told them not to take with them money or extra clothing in light of the teaching of the Old Testament. "For the worker is worth his keep" (Matthew 10:10). The Jews, who knew the Old Testament, understood that religious workers deserved to be supported. For that reason Jesus' disciples could expect to receive food and lodging when they worked among the Jews.

The apostles could not expect the same kind of reception when they went out to the Gentiles. They then needed financial support of another kind. Philippians 4:10–20 offers important teachings regarding the manner in which the first missionaries received material support.

PHILIPPIANS 4:10–20

The first thing we see when we look at this passage of Scripture is that Paul rejoiced when the Christians at Philippi showed *concern for him* (verse 10). They had benefited from his ministry in Philippi, and they were concerned about his needs when he went to other places. Their concern was evidence of their spiritual growth and sincerity, and it made Paul rejoice.

Paul admitted that he was *in need* (verse 11) and faced serious *troubles* (verse 14). He assured the Philippians that he had learned to be content in all kinds of circumstances and to depend on Christ for everything (verses 11–13). Nevertheless, Paul really did have material needs, and he was grateful that the Philippians came to his aid.

Paul praised the Christians at Philippi because, in contrast to other churches, they had supported him from the very beginning (verse 15). They were not slow to learn the importance of giving support to missions, but learned quickly. Paul went to Thessalonica to preach the gospel after he left Philippi. The Philippians continued to send financial and material support to him (verse 16). They had a heart for missions!

Paul was in prison in Rome when he wrote to the Philippians. He was blessed once again by gifts they sent him. He called their gifts "a fragrant offering, an acceptable sacrifice, pleasing to God" (verse 18). Paul assured the Philippians that God would be good to them just as they had been good to Paul (verse 19).

We learn some basic principles about the support of missions from this passage of Scripture. First, support should be given *in an organized way.* Paul sometimes suffered from lack of support because some churches either ignored his needs or the means of delivering help were not in place. The Philippians had good intentions, but for a time they had "no opportunity to show it" (verse 10).

The second lesson is that support should be collected in the churches and delivered to the missionaries *in an efficient and responsible manner.* Missionary boards and agencies are organized for the purpose of delivering the support of the churches into the hands of the missionaries where and when they are needed. Missionaries do not suffer unnecessarily when agencies do their work well.

A third lesson is that the support of missions is a *voluntary response of believers* who out of gratitude to God for salvation support the proclamation of the gospel. The Philippians voluntarily gave their gifts to support the missionary they loved. They were not paying a "tax" or trying to win favor with God.

Fourth, their support was more than adequate; it was *ample.* "I am amply supplied," said Paul (verse 18). The Christians at Philippi were not guilty of the false idea that missionaries could get along on almost nothing. The Philippians sent one of their own members, Epaphroditus, to deliver the gifts and stay with Paul and give him help in addition to material support.

Epaphroditus became very sick while he was with Paul, and Paul decided it was best to send him back to the church at Philippi. Paul praised Epaphroditus by saying that he was a man who had "almost died for the work of Christ, risking his life to make up for the help you could not give me" (Philippians 2:29–30).

A fifth lesson we can learn is that the support of missions should be carried out over the years *in a dependable manner.* Paul praised the Philippians for their faithful and dependable support (4:16). Other churches sometimes ignored the needs of the missionary (verse 15), but Paul could depend on the believers in Philippi. The Bible does not reveal the details of the system they used to raise support; but the results were clear, and the church was praised for its faithfulness.

Missionaries depend on faithful believers in whom they can have confidence, year after year, to support them with their prayers and their gifts. Those who support missionaries are true co-workers in the gospel.

Paul wrote in Philippians 1:4–5 about the prayers that he offered on behalf of the church. He prayed for them with great joy because of their "partnership in [the work of] the gospel." There is no greater privilege for any church, and for any believers, than to be partners with missionaries in proclaiming the gospel.

Finally, we can learn from this passage that the support of missionaries is a spiritual investment that God credits to the account of the givers (4:17). It is an offering presented not first of all to men, but to God (verse 18). All glory belongs to God, and he will richly reward those who support the work of missions (verses 19–20).

DOING EVERYTHING FOR THE SPREAD OF THE GOSPEL

Paul always feared that people would think he was serving as a missionary for personal gain. He assured the believers in Philippians 4:17 that he was not looking for a gift for himself, but for spiritual growth among them.

The apostle Paul reminded the believers in 1 Corinthians 9 that he had the right to receive support from them. He preferred to support himself, however, rather than give anyone the idea that he preached the gospel for personal profit.

> Don't we have the right to food and drink? . . . Or is it only I and Barnabas who must work for a living? . . . If others have this right of support from you, shouldn't we have it all the more? But we did not use this right. On the contrary, we put up with anything rather than hinder the gospel of Christ. . . . Woe to me if I do not

preach the gospel! If I preach voluntarily, I have a reward; if not voluntarily, I am simply discharging the trust committed to me. What then is my reward? Just this: that in preaching the gospel I may offer it free of charge, and so not make use of my rights in preaching it. (verses 4, 6, 12, 16–18)

The passion for souls that burned in the apostle's heart was so great that he was willing to do anything to spread the gospel. He was willing to become "a slave to everyone, to win as many as possible" (verse 19) even though he had many "rights." The financial support for missions is not a problem when that same kind of passion burns today in the hearts of missionaries and churches.

WHICH SYSTEM OF SUPPORT IS BEST?

There are various systems for supporting missions. The lessons we learned from the Scriptures should be observed whichever system is used.

Some missionaries receive financial support from a group of believers who are loyal to them personally and pray for them regularly. They may send their support through mission agencies that are organized for this purpose. The mission agencies also assist in recruiting missionaries in some cases, helping them go to the field and supervising their work.

Other missionaries receive support from one or more congregations. These congregations commit themselves to a certain amount of financial support each year. Paul and Barnabas returned to Antioch and told the church about their mission to the Gentiles (Acts 14:26–28). Likewise, missionaries visit the congregations that support them and inform them about their work. Missionaries stay in contact with their supporters by letters, phone calls, and e-mail. Contact of this kind encourages their continued support.

Denominations and groups of churches can provide missionaries with the support they need in an organized and dependable way. Denominations usually form their own agencies or boards of missions. These serve as the channels by which missionaries and their support go from the churches to the mission fields.

Systems of support will be different for churches and missionaries in different parts of the world. Churches are responsible to the Lord to develop systems that fit their cultures, needs, and situations. Certain principles should remain clear, whichever system of support is used.

- The financial support of missions is a basic and continual responsibility of churches everywhere.
- Missionaries should not be made to "beg" for support. They are not "second-class" workers who need and deserve less support than do pastors, teachers, and other workers.
- The system of support should permit missionaries to use as much of their time and energy as possible in mission work.
- All mission work is "by faith" from beginning to end. Whatever the system of support, missionaries have to trust in God and depend on the faithfulness of his people. Without faith, prayer, and sacrifice, all mission work will fail.

People in missions engage in an enterprise so great and difficult that it can be accomplished only by the power and will of God. Missionaries and those who support them, therefore, must be people of faith. Their faith will grow as they obey Christ's command, "Go and make disciples!"

Remember that the final goal of missions is that Christ will be known and worshipped everywhere. Those who do the work of missions in ways that honor Christ can be sure that he will supply their needs.

Review Questions

1. What is a "tentmaker," and what are the advantages and disadvantages of being a "tentmaker"?

2. What lessons about supporting missionaries do we learn in Philippians 4:10–20?

3. Why did Paul give up his "right" to support in Corinth?

4. What are the four principles of support given in this chapter?

Discussion Questions

1. Why do missionaries have to raise financial support?

2. What systems of financial support for Christian workers are you acquainted with? How well do they meet the needs?

3. How can financial support for missions be increased in your church?

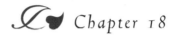 *Chapter 18*

The Ethics of
Evangelism and Missions

A Christian woman in a large office listened day after day as one of her co-workers told stories of how her husband mistreated her. The woman decided to share her own story, after some hesitation. She spoke with the abused woman and told how the Lord Jesus Christ had come into her life, and into the life of her family, bringing love and peace where before there was conflict. She urged her co-worker to ask Jesus to come into her life and into her husband's life.

The co-worker became very angry and accused the Christian woman of "proselytizing." The woman went to their supervisor and complained that her religious beliefs had been violated. She accused the Christian woman of trying to force religion on her. The supervisor warned the Christian employee that if it happened again she would be fired.

Things like this are happening more and more frequently. Evangelism, even of a humble and loving kind, makes some people angry. Christians are accused of invading the privacy of others when they witness to their faith. People say that we are arrogant because we believe Christ is the one and only way to God. They say that we fail to respect the sincere beliefs of others.

This raises questions such as the following:

- Are evangelism and missions ethical activities, or are they expressions of religious arrogance and aggression?
- Would it promote peace in the community if we said that all religions are equally valid and if we stopped all attempts to change the beliefs of other people?
- What is the difference between evangelism and proselytism?
- Are there rules that separate ethically legitimate from illegitimate methods of mission work?
- Is the call to conversion an insult to followers of other faiths?

These questions take us to the heart of the gospel. We will now examine these questions and look for biblical answers.

EVANGELISM CORRECTLY DEFINED

Evangelism is the communication of the good news about Jesus Christ in ways that invite a decision to either believe in him or reject him. The truth that Jesus is the one and only Savior and Lord is inherent in the gospel, and those who become his disciples give up their former gods and religious beliefs.

The goal of evangelism is, without question, conversion to Christ and repentance from all forms of idolatry. The apostle Paul made this clear when he said that his call to missions was to "open their eyes and turn them from darkness to light, and from the power of Satan to God, so that they may receive forgiveness of sins and a place among those who are sanctified by faith in [Christ]" (Acts 26:18).

It is not surprising that evangelism and missions are considered offensive and encounter opposition when they are defined in this way. Human hearts that have not yet been regenerated by the Holy Spirit reject the claims of Christ and are inclined to strike out at those who proclaim him.

Unpopular as evangelism may be, we should avoid the temptation to stay quiet about Christ, change the definition of evangelism, or substitute other activities for it. Instead, we should remember that Jesus, though he was sinless and did nothing but good to people, had bitter enemies. Paul was violently opposed. Christians throughout the centuries have been persecuted for witnessing to their faith. Given the nature of sin and the exclusive demands of the gospel, those who reject Christ will always find the message about Christ offensive.

Proselytism is different from evangelism in its character and methods. Proselytizers seek to win converts in order to glorify themselves and their group. Proselytizers use any method they can find to win converts. They may deceive by telling only part of the truth. They appeal to emotions and exploit muddled thinking. Proselytizers put converts in bondage to the leaders and rules of the group. The common motives behind proselytism are money and the power to control others.

METHODS TO AVOID

Jesus commanded that the gospel be proclaimed to all peoples, but he insisted on using methods that were ethical. Jesus never forced people to accept him, nor did he instruct his disciples to use methods designed to deceive people. Jesus openly and honestly told people what to expect if they followed him when he called them to become his disciples. He did not stir their emotions in order to make them follow him blindly and without thinking. Jesus clearly said that discipleship was costly. It meant cutting ties to people and things that belonged to this world; it meant bearing a cross (Luke 14:25–35).

Paul and other apostles in the first century already had to deal with people who were trying to advance the gospel by using deceitful and unethical methods. He assured the Corinthians, "We have renounced secret and shameful ways; we do not use deception, nor do we distort the word of God. On the contrary, by setting forth the truth plainly we commend ourselves to every man's conscience in the sight of God" (2 Corinthians 4:2). The implication was that certain other missionaries did not maintain the same standard. Paul put a distance between himself and them.

Being ethical, however, did not free the apostles from criticism and opposition. To the Thessalonians, Paul wrote,

> With the help of God we dared to tell you his gospel in spite of strong opposition. For the appeal we make does not spring from error or impure motives, nor are we trying to trick you. On the contrary, we speak as men approved by God to be entrusted with the gospel. We are not trying to please men but God, who tests our hearts. You know we never used flattery, nor did we put on a mask to cover up greed—God is our witness. We were not looking for praise from men, not from you or anyone else. As apostles of Christ we could have been a burden to you, but we were gentle among you, like a mother caring for her little children. (1 Thessalonians 2:2–7)

These scriptures make it plain that ethical behavior should characterize the words and actions of evangelists and missionaries. Their intentions must not be to serve themselves, and their methods should not be deceitful in any way. There should be no suggestion of obtaining personal benefits through spreading the gospel. The word of the gospel must be delivered above all else without change and without compromise.

ETHICAL GUIDELINES FOR EVANGELISTS

Moishe Rosen directed the missionary organization Jews for Jesus for many years. Because his evangelists were criticized

very often, Rosen carefully studied the apostle Paul's writings
and example in matters of ethical conduct in mission work. At
a meeting of the Lausanne Consultation on Jewish Evangelism
in Dallas, Texas, in 1985, Rosen proposed the following ethical
guidelines for evangelists:

- The gospel should be proclaimed in ways that please
  God by conforming to his Word and not in ways de-
  signed to please the hearers.
- Gospel proclamation should not involve any kind of de-
  ception.
- Any suggestion that greed motivates the evangelist is
  entirely unacceptable.
- All the glory should be to God in evangelism, and no
  glory should be given to the proclaimers.
- Godly evangelists do not demand their rights, but their
  principal concern is the welfare of their hearers.
- Godly evangelism is gentle and does not use force of
  any kind.
- Evangelism of the kind that pleases God comes from
  sincere love toward those it seeks to win to Christ.
- The basis of true evangelism is love for our neighbors,
  that is, seeking after their highest good.

Rosen says that in Christian evangelism the end never jus-
tifies the means. We must be gentle in the way we proclaim
spiritual information so powerful that it can make eternal
changes in the hearts and lives of our hearers. Our faith is in a
sovereign God whose message of salvation we proclaim. Therefore, we avoid methods of persuasion that show disrespect for
men and women. We regard our hearers as people created in
the image of God, and ultimately we are responsible to him for
their decisions and actions.

The basic motive for ethical conduct in evangelism is not
to avoid criticism but to honor the Lord and obey his will. Opposition is not going to disappear even though missionaries

and evangelists speak and act with delicate care. The Spirit of God alone can bring conviction and repentance. All success depends on the Spirit.

IS IT ETHICAL TO EXPECT CONVERSION?

Dr. Mahendra Singhal is a professor of mathematics at a university in the United States. Dr. Singhal told the story of his conversion from Hinduism to Christ in an article entitled "The Cost of Conversion," published in *World Evangelization* (vol. 15, no. 53). He wrote,

> When I converted to Christianity, my father an-
> nounced that so far as he was concerned, I had never
> been born. The reaction of my mother was not as vio-
> lent as that of my father. She was totally submissive
> and fearful of him, and there was nothing she could
> do to defend me. In India, conversion to Christ
> means that you lose your status in society. You become
> an "untouchable," and to be an untouchable means
> you do not mix with the upper castes. In most cases it
> means that your own family will have nothing more to
> do with you.

Dr. Singhal described the fear and frustration that exist side by side in the hearts of devout Hindus. They are afraid of reincarnation on the one hand, with its possibility of re-turning to a life of worse suffering. On the other hand they feel frustrated because they never can achieve any assur-ance of satisfying the demands of whatever gods they wor-ship.

When he first heard the gospel, Dr. Singhal found it radi-cally different from anything taught in Hinduism. He thought Christians were arrogant, because they claimed that through faith in Christ they had the assurance of going to heaven.

After many discussions, Bible study, and the testimony of Indian Christians whose lives gave evidence of the grace of God, Mahendra Singhal converted and openly professed faith in Christ. Trouble began when he informed his family. His father became furious and never forgave him. He had reason to believe that his uncle tried to poison him. Old friends treated him as a traitor.

The cost of conversion to Christianity can be extremely high in many societies. It may bring divisions within the family and the loss of employment and reputation in the community. It may even cost converts their lives.

These question then arise: Is it ethical for missionaries and evangelists to call people to conversion? Is it too much to ask? If conversion brings so much pain with it, is the missionary call to convert to Christ morally justified in view of the trouble and opposition that conversion can cause?

These questions force us to think about the core of Christianity. If what the Bible teaches is true—through Christ alone human beings can find salvation, because Christ is the only divine-human Mediator who came, died, arose, reigns, and will return—then the answer is clear. Not only is the call to convert to Christ ethical, but it is *unethical not to evangelize.* We offer people the only hope they can have of knowing God, receiving his forgiveness, and enjoying peace with him. Evangelism and mission work are an *ethical obligation.*

REVIEW QUESTIONS

1. Describe the characteristics of proselytism.

2. Describe the characteristics of evangelism.

3. Show how 1 Thessalonians 2:2–7 guides true evangelists.

DISCUSSION QUESTIONS

1. Is "sheep stealing" between churches ever ethical? Explain.

2. How would you counsel a new convert to Christ whose family is very dedicated to the convert's former religion?

3. How would you defend evangelism against charges of "arrogance" and "religious imperialism"?

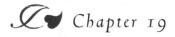 *Chapter 19*

Missions and Unity Among Christians

Jesus said, "Blessed are the peacemakers, for they will be called sons of God" (Matthew 5:9). Peacemakers are urgently needed in a divided world filled with hatred and conflicts.

Missionaries are called to be peacemakers. They proclaim Christ, the Great Peacemaker between God and sinners. The Bible calls Christ the "Prince of Peace" (Isaiah 9:6). The apostle Paul was inspired by the Holy Spirit to describe the peace, unity, and reconciliation that Christ brings.

> For he [Christ] is our peace, who has made the two one [Gentiles and Jews] and has destroyed the barrier, the dividing wall of hostility, by abolishing in his flesh the law with its commandments and regulations. His purpose was to create in himself one new man out of the two, thus making peace, and in this one body to reconcile both of them to God through the cross, by which he put to death their hostility. He came and preached peace to you who were far away and peace to those who were near. For through him we both have access to the Father by one Spirit. (Ephesians 2:14–18)

THE GLOBAL FRUIT OF MISSIONS

The church of Christ has become the largest fellowship of people in the world. This fellowship consists of people of all races, nationalities, cultures, and languages. More people became Christians and more churches were started in the twentieth century than in any previous century. It will grow even more in the twenty-first century, by the grace of God.

Christians around the world profess to be united in the Body of Christ. We remember Christ's death for the sins of all believers at the Table of Holy Communion. We profess that we share "one Lord, one faith, one baptism" (Ephesians 4:5). We look forward to being together in heaven where we will worship God forever in one, united assembly (Revelation 5:9–10).

WHY ON EARTH ARE CHRISTIANS DIVIDED?

If it is true that Christians form one, global, spiritual fellowship, why are there divisions and conflicts between us, and why are they permitted to continue? Why do churches split over minor disagreements? Why do churches segregate along lines of race, tribe, caste, or social class?

Have we forgotten that unity among believers contributes to the spread of the gospel but disunity damages missions? Jesus said in his great prayer shortly before his arrest and crucifixion,

> My prayer is not for them [the disciples] alone. I pray also for those who will believe in me through their message, that all of them may be one, Father, just as you are in me and I am in you. May they also be in us so that the world may believe that you have sent me. I have given them the glory that you gave me, that they may be one as we are one: I in them and you in me. May they be brought to complete unity to let the world

know that you sent me and have loved them as you
have loved me. (John 17:20–23)

A vital part of the work of missionaries, in view of what
Christ taught and prayed for, ought to be bringing an end to
conflicts and divisions between Christians. The apostle Paul
made it part of his work (1 Corinthians 3:1–9), and the need is
equally great now.

Missionaries must be peacemakers in every sense of the
word. They must make it clear when they preach the gospel
that all people, races, tribes, and castes have one Creator. God
the Creator made everyone in his image (Genesis 1:26–27).
The great tragedy of the human race is that all have sinned and
earned for themselves the judgment of God (Genesis 3:16–19;
Romans 3:23; 6:23). That is how hostilities, conflicts, and divisions began. First there was separation from God, and then followed divisions between people.

God is reconciling sinners to himself, however, through the
saving work of Jesus Christ and by the preaching of the gospel
(2 Corinthians 5:18–21). All we who by faith are joined to
Christ form one body of redeemed and reconciled people.
This gospel of reconciliation through Christ is our message to
the world. We must proclaim it by our actions as well as our
words.

DAMAGE TO MISSIONS AND WHY IT CONTINUES

Consider these three cases:

(1) There was a pastor who had great gifts in evangelism in
a country in southern Asia where I ministered for a time. God
used him to draw many people to Christ. Yet some members of
the church continually attacked him for one reason or another.
The pastor finally left the ministry of that denomination.

What was the real problem? Some of us knew the pastor
well, and we respected him highly. We also knew the situation

in the church, and we understood what lay behind the conflict. The fact was that the pastor was of a different ethnic group than most of the members. Nothing the pastor did could please some of the members because of his ethnic identity. Ethnic identity was more important to them than Christian identity. The unity of believers in the Body of Christ meant practically nothing to them.

(2) I met a veteran missionary in a West African country who had a serious problem. This missionary had a powerful ministry of prayer, and through prayer and Bible studies he had won a number of educated Muslims to Christ. Conflict arose when the converts came to church. The members of the church were of a different tribe, and Muslims had persecuted them in the past. They did not want to receive the new converts into their church. They began to criticize the missionary for different reasons, and eventually they forced him to leave the area.

(3) A division occurred in a North American congregation that involved three levels of controversy. First, there was controversy over where to erect a new building. One group wanted to tear down the old building and put up a new building on the same property. Another group wanted to buy land some distance away and put up a building there.

Second, one group wanted other changes along with a new location. This group came to be regarded as "liberal" in theology. They wanted changes in the worship services and in the way the minister preached. They wanted more evangelism and new ministries for young people. They also wanted a building that would be adequate for these ministries.

Third, the conflict had to do with members who wanted power. Certain members had always controlled the church, and they intended to remain in control. The church divided after many months of conflict, the pastor left, and many people were hurt.

Something might have been done to reconcile the opposing sides in each of these cases, but nobody acted in time. Why do we permit conflicts to continue when they harm us and our witness to the world? Some reasons are the following:

- Most of us try to avoid becoming involved with people who are in conflict with one another, especially when they are brothers and sisters in Christ, pastors, and missionaries.
- Few of us have learned the skills of identifying the problems, resolving conflicts, and healing the wounds that conflicts cause.
- Most Christians are ashamed of the conflicts and hope that if they ignore them they will disappear.
- Some Christians assume that nothing can be done to solve conflicts.

CASES OF CONFLICT IN THE NEW TESTAMENT

There will always be conflicts because this is a sinful world and even the lives of Christians are not perfect. Missionaries in particular confront differences between cultures, traditions, and ways of living that easily produce conflicts. Missionaries need to prepare themselves to become peacemakers between Christians as well as peacemakers between unbelievers and God. They must have faith that with the help of the Holy Spirit, many conflicts can be resolved if wise steps are taken on time.

There are a number of examples of conflicts between Christians in the New Testament in the context of missions, and each of them offers us instruction.

1. Acts 6:1–7

Conflict broke out very early in the life of the church over what appeared to be the unjust way some widows were treated. This might have led to a very serious division in the church;

but it was handled wisely and quickly, and the gospel continued to spread as a result (verse 7).

2. Galatians 2:11–21

Paul and Peter had a face-to-face confrontation. The truth of the gospel was put in jeopardy by Peter's behavior. Paul confronted Peter boldly. The Bible does not say precisely how the conflict was resolved, but it appears that Peter accepted the rebuke and repented from his error.

3. Acts 15:1–35

There was "sharp dispute and debate" at Antioch caused by some men from Judea over the need for circumcision. They raised questions that threatened the truth of the gospel as preached by Paul and others. The conflict was resolved (a) by sending it to a "higher court," the broader assembly of Christian leaders at Jerusalem (verse 2), and later (b) by accepting the decision that was made in Jerusalem as being the will of God (verses 30–31).

4. Acts 15:36–41

There was "sharp disagreement" between the two missionaries, Paul and Barnabas, over whether to give John Mark a second chance. Separation from each other appeared to be the only solution.

5. Philippians 4:2–3

Euodia and Syntyche were two women who had helped Paul in spreading the gospel, and they were in serious disagreement with cach other. The Bible does not tell us the cause of their disagreement. It appears that it was not over doctrine or morality. How does Paul address the conflict? He names them by name and pleads with them to "agree with each other in the Lord" (verse 2). He reminds them of the good times they had when they worked with Paul. He also asks that the local pastor or elder, his "loyal yokefellow" (verse 3), actively intervene by helping the two women put an end to their disagreement. Paul knew how dangerous and damaging it was to let conflicts like this continue.

6. Conflicts and Divisions in the Church at Corinth

Paul's two letters to the church at Corinth show that they had serious conflicts and divisions. Groups within the church chose different leaders and took sides (1 Corinthians 1–2). They clashed over whether Paul was really a "first-class" apostle (1 Corinthians 3; 2 Corinthians 11). The leaders were slow to address immorality in the church, perhaps because important people were guilty (1 Corinthians 4–5). Rich members provoked divisions by showing off their fine food when the congregation ate together (1 Corinthians 11:17–22), and some even got drunk at these dinners (verse 21).

Clearly, even as the New Testament was being written, the church was experiencing conflicts. Some of the conflicts were between Jewish and gentile believers, others were between believers who had different views on the Christian life, and still others were between leaders. Much of the apostles' work had to do with resolving these conflicts. Their writing and example show us ways to deal with conflicts in churches and missions in our time.

SUGGESTIONS FOR MISSIONARIES AND OTHER LEADERS

First, we must accept the fact that missionaries and other church leaders have to live with high levels of tension among the people they serve. Conflicts are unavoidable. Along with the call to leadership, we accept the responsibility of dealing with differences and misunderstandings, and in some cases with very difficult people.

Second, we must work hard in every situation in which we minister to build and maintain a network of people with whom we are in regular contact. New missionaries especially should make serious efforts to become acquainted with a large number of local people and earn their confidence.

Communication between leaders, workers, and regular members is essential. Conflicts that develop can be resolved more easily if a strong network of trust and communication is already established.

Third, as leaders we should use every opportunity to emphasize the beliefs, values, and spiritual unity that bind us together with other Christians. We can promote peace and reconciliation by our writing, teaching, and casual conversation, and stop the spread of misunderstanding and conflict. We can remind Christians of what the Bible teaches on subjects where there are differences of opinion. We encourage them in this way to examine the differences by the light of eternal truth instead of merely by their traditions and prejudices.

Fourth, as peacemakers we must not run away from serious conflicts when they occur. We should do our best to resolve them and bring reconciliation. The process of reconciliation involves looking closely at (1) the reasons behind the conflicts; (2) what the parties in the conflict are really seeking; (3) who may have been injured and what were the causes of the offense; and (4) what influences from outside may have contributed to the conflict. People are required to repent, ask for forgiveness, and seek reconciliation when they have spoken or acted wrongly.

Fifth, if one side or the other says that the conflict is doctrinal and theological, be very careful. If indeed it is a matter of theology, it must be examined carefully in the light of the Bible. False doctrines may not be permitted. Be aware that people who are involved in a conflict may try to make it appear to be a conflict over doctrine in order to strengthen their own side. The real cause may not be theological at all, but a struggle for power or a difference of opinion over some practical matter.

Keep in mind that conflicts are usually very complicated. Do not try to find a single, simple solution, because that will only lead to more difficulties later on. Remember that there is seldom a "perfect" solution that satisfies everybody. Perfect solutions are found only in heaven. Strive for unity with patience and love in matters that do not affect sound doctrine.

Building and maintaining unity among believers is not an easy task. It is especially difficult in intercultural missions where misunderstandings so easily arise over cultural differences. Remember that Satan is a deceiver and a divider, and he continually tries to reduce the power of Christian testimony. We must pray that unity among believers be established and maintained for the welfare of the church and the advancement of missions.

REVIEW QUESTIONS

1. Give evidence that mission work is fruitful.

2. Why is Jesus concerned for unity among his followers?

3. Why do many Christians avoid dealing with conflicts?

4. In what two ways are missionaries "peacemakers"?

DISCUSSION QUESTIONS

1. Who is the Great Peacemaker in Ephesians 2:14–18, and what are the practical implications of the passage today?

2. Give examples from your experience of the kinds of conflicts that were found already in the days of the apostles.

3. Discuss the practical suggestions offered in this chapter,
and select two that you think are especially important.

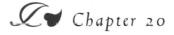 *Chapter 20*

Preparing to
Become a Missionary

I remember hearing the famous missionary to Hindus, E. Stanley Jones, say to a group of students gathered in Mexico City,

> Some of you young people are thinking about the ministry and missions. My advice to you is this: If you can stay out, stay out; but if you cannot stay out, come in! It is wonderful!

There is only one calling for Christians, to follow Christ in service to the glory of God and the growth of his kingdom; but there are various assignments within the one calling. I have some advice based on more than forty years of experience for those who are called to become missionaries.

MISSIONARIES ARE BUILDERS

The apostle Paul called himself an expert builder (1 Corinthians 3:10). The buildings he worked on were churches of Jesus Christ (verse 9). The foundation was the person and work of Jesus Christ (verse 11). Everything depended on that foundation.

Paul knew that he did not work alone. Other believers worked along with him, and many more would come after him. The question for all builders is the same: *What is the quality of your work* (verse 13)? Will the work of the builders endure, or will it fall down in the time of testing?

We know that builders need the right tools in order to do good work. Watch an excellent carpenter use his tools! He knows exactly which tools he needs for each project. Builders are limited in what they can do without the right tools. However, with the right tools, they can build things that are beautiful and lasting.

The application to mission work is obvious. All who want to work for God need to acquire the right tools, and they must learn how to use them. "Tools" are the knowledge of the Word of God and the spiritual qualities and experiences that are necessary for Christian work.

Below I list many of the tools that, in my experience, are necessary for fruitful mission work. Nobody has all the tools, nor does every worker need all the tools at all times. I promise you, however, that you will certainly need most of the tools in the course of your ministry. Some of the tools you will need right from the start.

All those who want to be used to build the church of Christ through mission work should begin early to gather the tools they will need. Do not wait until you begin your first missionary assignment. Acquire as many tools as you can as early as you can, and learn how to use them well.

You can be sure that missionary service will test the quality of your Christian character. It will test your abilities more than you expect now. Start now, and make every effort to build your skills for ministry. Gain experience in serving the Lord. If you are married, or plan to be married, include your spouse in the process of learning to use the right tools for missions.

BASIC MISSIONARY TOOLS

1. *Strong Spiritual Life*

This includes the daily discipline of prayer and Bible reading in the fellowship of the Holy Spirit. There are many urgent things to do in missions, and the workers are few. Missionaries are tempted to become very involved in many good and important ministries but neglect their spiritual life.

In a survey taken among missionaries in more than a dozen countries, spiritual weakness was identified as their number-one problem. Many of the missionaries admitted that they had not developed the habit of daily private prayer and Bible reading before going into missions. Their spiritual life suffered greatly once in the work.

The best advice I can give to anyone preparing to become a missionary is to enter missions on your knees. Missionaries experience loneliness, temptation, satanic attacks, and periods of depression and disappointment. Master the spiritual tools of Bible reading, prayer, worship, and communion with God before anything else.

2. *Love for People*

Paul is an example of a loving missionary. He wrote to the Christians at Philippi that he had them "in my heart" (Philippians 1:7). The Bible says that the leaders of the church at Ephesus "all wept as they embraced him and kissed him" when Paul said farewell (Acts 20:37). Paul's great love for people as well as for God was at the center of his success as an evangelist and church planter.

Unfortunately, some Christians like books and privacy more than they love people. They want to serve the Lord, but they do not want to get close to people. Mission work, however, requires becoming involved with all kinds of people and loving them for the sake of Christ.

I was invited by a pastor in Mexico to help him discover what was wrong in the Sunday school of his church. The leader of the Sunday school was a highly educated person and seemed to be dedicated to organizing an excellent program. There was one problem after another, however, in the Sunday school. Everyone became frustrated.

I visited the classes and talked with the superintendent for several hours. I discovered the root of the problem when the superintendent told me, "I find great pleasure in organizing and leading the Sunday school. But keep the children away from me. I do not like children!"

Here was the reason for all the problems in the Sunday school. The person in charge did not love the children! Sometimes there are missionaries who do not love the people whom they are trying to lead to Christ. Some pastors do not love their congregations. Such people do not bless Christian work.

Ask God to give you great love for people of all kinds as you think about becoming a missionary. Spend time with people. Learn to understand them, and look for ways to serve them for the sake of Christ. Love is essential in missions.

3. A Biblical Theology of Missions

We will not fulfill the calling of God in missions unless we have a basic understanding of God's saving purpose for the world as revealed in the Bible. Missions receives its inspiration and direction from the Scriptures. Missionaries must continually study the Bible, or they may be carried away by ideas that come in the name of "missions" but are for the most part false.

Be sure to gain a firm foundation in the Scriptures before going out as a missionary, and stay close to the Word throughout your life. Pass on to new believers and to the leaders of the churches with whom you work the biblical basis for missions that you yourself embrace. You will build their faith and inspire them to missions.

4. Goals and Strategies

Wise carpenters follow a plan when they build a house. They do not simply nail boards together hoping that in some way a house will result from their efforts. Instead, they produce the kind of building they want by following a plan.

Sometimes Christians make the mistake of thinking that plans are not necessary in mission work. That is foolishness.

Missionaries need to set biblical goals, such as planting churches among people who do not have a church and expanding the kingdom of Christ by helping poor people become productive and able to earn a living. Missionaries must also follow biblical methods in achieving their goals. The Bible is filled with examples to guide us. Careful plans, humbly submitted to God in prayer, receive his blessing.

5. Training and Experience in the Following Areas

- *Personal evangelism.* Missionaries need to be able to tell the story of the gospel, of the saving work of God in Christ, clearly, accurately, and in ways that their hearers can understand.
- *Organized evangelism.* Missionaries very often work as a team. Learn to work with others, therefore, in carrying out organized mission activity.
- *Small group Bible studies.* Small group Bible studies are the most effective method for spreading the gospel in countries and cultures throughout the world. Learn how to organize and lead them at home before going to some other place.
- *Counseling and teaching new disciples.* New converts need help in dealing with problems rooted in their old lives. They need instruction in the basic Christian disciplines of prayer, worship, baptism, service, and morality. Missionaries must be prepared to teach these.

- *The organization of the church and its ministry.* The apostle Paul gave us an example by organizing churches wherever he could. Be active in a good church, and learn how it is organized and how it functions before you become a missionary. Learn all you can from the pastors.
- *Developing leaders.* Gain experience in leadership by taking responsibility for different kinds of ministry. You will train others to become leaders later when you are a missionary.
- *Helping the poor.* Christians are always required to help the poor, and as a missionary you will probably meet many poor people. Learn how to help the poor in such a way that they become free of dependence upon charity.

6. Adjustment to Other Cultures and Societies

Mission work very often requires that missionaries go to live among people of a different culture and language as well as religion. Success in mission work depends to a large extent on the willingness and ability of missionaries to make social and cultural changes in their lives.

Spend time living and working among people who are different from you as part of your preparation for missionary service. Seek for opportunities to test whether you possess the gifts and attitudes necessary for living and working in other cultures.

7. If Married, a Spouse Who Is Committed to Missions

Stress and sacrifice come with missions. Both the husband and the wife need to be certain that they are following the will of God when they go into missions.

If you have children, their needs must be considered carefully. Failure to meet the needs of the family is one of the most common reasons why missionaries return home earlier than they planned.

Having a family with you in missions can advance the gospel, or it can hold the gospel back. Therefore, think carefully about the family as you make plans for missionary service.

8. *Your Gifts and Personality*

God has made each of us different, and he uses all kinds of people. Missionaries are often expected to be willing and able to do everything. This can lead to anxiety and unhappiness.

Gain experience in a variety of work areas, and learn what your gifts are before going into missions. What kind of work gives you the most satisfaction? Look for a mission agency that can assign you to work that matches your gifts and personality.

ENTHUSIASM FOR THE LORD AND FOR MISSIONS

I hope that all who feel called to missions feel a deep enthusiasm for the Lord Jesus Christ and for the ministry of the gospel. *"It is wonderful!"* as E. Stanley Jones said. There is no deeper satisfaction than that which missionaries experience when they see the Spirit of God changing hearts and lives and working through their weak efforts to build churches of Christ.

REVIEW QUESTIONS

1. List the principal "tools" missionaries need and briefly explain each of them.

2. Where can we go to learn about "goals and strategies"? Give examples.

3. What is the single most effective and adaptable method for spreading the gospel?

DISCUSSION QUESTIONS

1. Why is working with churches important in missions?

2. How do short-term missions play a role in preparing people for long-term missionary service?

3. What special gifts has God given you that you might use in missionary service?

 *Appendix*

How to Evangelize and Multiply Churches

Many years ago I published a small book in the Spanish language entitled *6 Pasos: Como evangelizar y multiplicar iglesias* ("Six Steps: How to evangelize and multiply churches"). The Holy Spirit used that small book to inspire students, pastors, and lay people to follow its simple steps and start churches. One person in South America began twenty-five churches by following the instructions of the book.

I present the main ideas of "Six Steps" here as an appendix at the suggestion of Harold Kallemeyn, missionary to French-speaking peoples. I hope that it will motivate those who read *Go and Make Disciples!* to engage in the kind of evangelism that multiplies churches of Jesus Christ.

INTRODUCTION

Men and women desire to share their faith with others when the Holy Spirit fills their hearts with living faith. This desire comes from God, who wants people everywhere to know him and be saved (1 Timothy 2:4).

The motive for evangelism comes from the Spirit of God who lives in every believer. The Spirit gives men and women power to do what they cannot do in their own strength wherever they are moved by the Spirit to bring the gospel to others. The Spirit opens doors before them and leads them to people whom God intends to draw to himself (John 6:44).

There is joy in the work of evangelism when sinners repent and come to God. There are also disappointments when people refuse to listen to the message of Christ and reject the messengers. There may also be suffering and persecution when Satan and his servants try to stop the spread of the gospel.

This instruction is for you if you desire to be the instrument of God to draw others to Christ and build his church. The New Testament teaches that Paul and the other apostles preached the gospel and established churches wherever they went. They did not consider the work of evangelism complete until a congregation of believers was established.

In addition to the apostles, many other believers evangelized and started churches. The majority of the churches in the first century were started by lay Christians who, empowered by the Holy Spirit, worked hard to spread the gospel.

The steps you find below are basically the same steps that the apostles and others followed. I studied the Bible, prayed for divine light on the work of missions, and tried many different methods over many years. I found that these are the steps that produce the most fruit with the blessing of God.

I believe that if you follow these same steps, God will use your efforts to draw people to Christ and multiply churches. May the Spirit of God bless you with power in the proclamation of his Word and with fruit that will endure for eternity.

STEP 1. START A BIBLE STUDY

How to Begin

Begin with prayer for God's direction and for the power of the Holy Spirit. Pray for open doors and open hearts. Pray for the people whom you expect to invite. Pray that God will be glorified by the work you intend to do.

Whom to Invite

Invite your friends, members of your family, neighbors who are not Christians, and all who show interest in the Christian message to your Bible study.

When and Where to Meet

Choose a time that is convenient to the majority of people you hope will attend. Find a place where there will be few interruptions or disturbances.

What to Do in the Meeting

You or another believer should serve as the leader in the meeting. Do not be too formal. Follow these suggestions:

1. Explain in a few words that you have invited them for the purpose of enjoying a time of fellowship, praying for each other's needs, and studying the teachings of the Bible.

2. Lead in prayer, asking for divine help and for understanding the Bible.

3. Read a passage from the Bible that you have carefully chosen beforehand. It is wise to begin with one of the Gospels and study the same Gospel each week.

4. Explain the Bible passage, answering the following four questions:

- First, what did these words say to the first people who heard them?
- Second, what do they say to us about God and his will?
- Third, what can we learn from them about Jesus?
- Fourth, how should we obey what they teach?

Then, invite anyone in the group to ask questions about the passage and how they should apply it to their lives.

5. Choose a hymn or chorus and sing together. Teach new people how to sing Christian songs.

6. Invite everyone to talk about their needs and concerns, and then pray for them. Ask believers who are growing in faith to pray for others in the group.

7. Invite those who may have additional questions or personal problems to talk to you after the meeting.

8. Announce the time and place of the next meeting, and encourage each person to bring a friend or family member to the meeting next time.

9. Serve tea, coffee, and refreshments before the group departs.

What to Do Between Meetings

1. Encourage all who attend to read one or two chapters of the Bible every day and pray to God in the name of Jesus Christ. Prayers should include the following:

- thanks for the blessings of God,
- confession of sins,
- request for pardon and cleansing,
- petition for God's direction and understanding of his will for our lives,
- intercession for other people and their needs.

2. Encourage all who attend to obey the commandments of God and live in peace with their neighbors.

STEP 2. VISIT HOMES

The Importance of Visiting Homes

Few things are more important than making personal visits to the homes of people who show interest in the gospel and attend the Bible studies. You should omit such visits only in cases where there is severe opposition to the gospel by other members of the family.

Visits in the Home Serve in the Following Ways

1. You learn to know the other members of the family and build friendly relations with them.

2. You demonstrate your interest in each member of the home with his or her needs and burdens, and you show your willingness to help if you can.

3. You have the opportunity to speak to family members personally about their need for the Savior Jesus Christ, explain the way of salvation to them, and pray with them.

How to Visit Homes

1. *Begin with prayer.* Pray to God before you go out to visit that he will use your visits to glorify his name and draw people to Jesus Christ.

2. *Take your Bible.* You do not know what opportunities await you to teach the way of salvation directly from the Word of God. Therefore, go prepared.

3. *Visit homes at an appropriate time.* Visit homes when members of the family are in the house, but not at meal time. You want to meet all the members of the family and gain their interest and good will. Men should never enter a house when a woman is there alone. Women should not enter homes where only men are present.

4. *Show interest in the life and needs of the family.* If there are serious needs, try to help them. Show Christian love by what you do as well as by what you say.

5. *Speak the Word of the Lord.* Remember that you are in the home as the servant and messenger of God. Read or recite some verses from the Bible that speak to the family's situation and explain what they mean. If they have questions, try to answer them.

6. *Ask them to let you pray.* If someone is sick, pray for healing. Ask God to meet the needs of each person in the home, and above all, give them faith in Jesus.

7. *Show hope and joy.* Some people in the home may be negative toward you. Show them by your words and attitude that you have hope and joy in Christ. Tell them that you will pray for them and that they may call you for prayer when they have a crisis in their lives.

8. *Invite everyone to the Bible study.* Personal invitations are powerful. Many people will never attend until they receive a personal invitation. You may invite some people many times without response. Nevertheless, continue to invite them.

9. *Guide them to faith in Christ.* Faith in Christ may begin during a Bible study, or during your visit to the home, or afterwards when people are alone. Some people decide to follow Christ quickly and suddenly, while it is a slow process for others. When you visit homes, look for signs that God is working in people's hearts. Be ready to explain the plan of salvation by grace through faith in Christ, and lead them in prayer for forgiveness and membership in the family of God. Invite people who are converted to Christ during a visit in the home to testify at the next Bible study.

What Can You Expect?

When you visit homes, witness for Christ, and start Bible studies, what can you expect to see happen?

1. The Lord by his Spirit will work in the hearts of some of the people. Their faith in Christ will grow, and they will praise God for his mercy.

2. The feeling will grow among them that they are a group of believers in Christ and followers of his Word. They will feel attached to one another and to their leader.

3. Some will lose interest and stop attending the meetings. Others will remain faithful. New people will be added and become believers. The new people often will be more dedicated than those who first attended.

4. Some will want more instruction in Christian teaching. You will know that the time has come for the third step when you see this. Continue giving Bible studies and visiting the homes, and add a class in Christian discipleship.

STEP 3. BEGIN A CLASS IN DISCIPLESHIP

What Is "Discipleship"?

Remember Jesus' missionary command: *Go and make DISCIPLES!* Jesus explained what he meant by adding the instructions, (1) *baptizing them in the name of the Father, the Son, and the Holy Spirit;* and (2) *teaching them to obey everything I have commanded you* (Matthew 28:19–20).

Jesus' disciples know who the true God is and how he saves those people who believe in him through Jesus. Disciples listen to the Word of God and follow it. "To make" disciples means to inform people about God and about the life, death, and resurrection of Jesus.

Being a disciple means growing in understanding the Word of God and trying to do what it teaches with the strength that the Holy Spirit provides.

Discipleship means worshipping God, praying to him, obeying his commandments, studying the Bible, serving the needs of others, being part of the fellowship of the church, and telling unbelievers about salvation through Christ.

Discipleship means putting off the "old self, which is being corrupted by its deceitful desires," and, by the power the Holy Spirit gives, putting on the "new self, created to be like God in true righteousness and holiness" (Ephesians 4:22–24).

Whom to Invite to a Class in Discipleship

Invite those who attend the Bible studies, who show that they are interested in learning more about the teachings of the Bible, and who desire to be baptized.

When and Where to Meet

Teach the class at a time that is convenient to those who desire to attend. It may be necessary for you to give more than one class each week if people have busy schedules. Give the class in a place where you will not be interrupted or disturbed.

Who Should Teach the Class?

Usually, the person who teaches the Bible study also teaches the class in discipleship, but the teacher can be some other Christian. Teachers must prepare well, with much prayer and study. They must remember that the teachings of the Word of God have eternal consequences for the lives of the people who hear them. The Bible says, "Faith comes from hearing the message, and the message is heard through the word of Christ" (Romans 10:17).

What Should Be Studied?

We have already said what it means to be a disciple of Christ. Study what the Bible teaches about this. Your church may have a book with the basic doctrines of the Bible that you can use in the class.

How Long Should the Class Continue?

Encourage everyone in the class to continue until they have studied the major doctrines about God, salvation, and the Christian life. Those who then desire to be baptized and become members of the church can do so.

Classes can be offered after that to new people who desire to learn the Word of God and follow Jesus.

STEP 4. BAPTIZE THE BELIEVERS, AND IF POSSIBLE THEIR ENTIRE HOUSEHOLDS

Why Is Baptism Important?

Baptism is important because Jesus commanded it, saying, "Therefore go and make disciples of all nations, *baptizing them in the name of the Father and of the Son and of the Holy Spirit*" (Matthew 28:19).

Who Should Be Baptized?

All who have repented from their sins, believe in Christ as their Lord and Savior, and promise to live according to the teachings of Christ should be baptized.

The entire family should be baptized if they are prepared for this important step, following the example of the apostle Paul in Acts 16:33.

Who Should Do the Baptizing?

Churches have learned by experience that baptism must be protected from misuse. Most churches, therefore, require that baptism be done by a pastor who examines the people who desire to be baptized concerning their faith and commitment to Christ.

How and Where Should Baptisms Be Done?

1. Baptisms should be done in a place where the ones to be baptized offer a testimony to everyone about wanting to follow Jesus.

2. Baptisms should be performed with water on the head or by immersion in a river, a lake, or an ocean, as a sign of the washing away of sin by the blood of Christ and the beginning of a new life in him.

3. Baptisms should be proclaimed in the name of the triune God, the Father, Son, and Holy Spirit.

4. Baptisms should be accompanied by the reading of Scripture and the preaching of the gospel.

The Change That Baptism Signifies

People who are baptized enter into a new and eternal relationship with the triune God, Father, Son, and Holy Spirit. Baptism means the end of the old life of sin and the beginning of the new life of love and obedience to God. The Bible says in Romans 6:1–4,

> What shall we say, then? Shall we go on sinning so that grace may increase? By no means! We died to sin; how can we live in it any longer? Or don't you know that all of us who were baptized into Christ Jesus were baptized into his death? We were therefore buried with him through baptism into death in order that, just as Christ was raised from the dead through the glory of the Father, we too may live a new life.

STEP 5. ORGANIZE A CHURCH

The church, as we see it on earth, is the Body of Christ organized in local assemblies of believers and their children.

We should not leave new believers in isolation from other Christians if we follow the teaching and example of the apostles. We gather believers into congregations wherever possible. These are communities of faith, fellowship, and service to God. They are usually called "churches."

Who May Become Members of the Church?

1. All who profess their faith in Jesus Christ as Savior and Lord and are baptized in the name of the triune God.

2. All who agree with the basic doctrines of the Bible concerning God, salvation, and the Christian life on which the church is established.

3. Believers who come from other Christian churches and fulfill the requirements given above.

4. Entire families of believers when they are baptized. It is wonderful to see how God works from one generation to another. What God promised Abraham, the father of all believers (Romans 4:11), remains true.

> I will establish my covenant as an everlasting covenant between me and you and your descendants after you for the generations to come, to be your God and the God of your descendants after you. (Genesis 17:7)

Characteristics of a Strong and Healthy Church

1. The Word of God, the Bible, is preached regularly and the members come together faithfully to receive its instruction.

2. Baptism and the Holy Communion are administered regularly, with instruction as to their meaning from the Word of God.

3. The members of the church live according to the Word of God. If members depart from the way of truth and righteousness, other members plead with them to repent and change their ways. If they refuse to repent, they are removed from the church.

4. Prayer is a vital part of the life of the church and its members. There is more in the New Testament about praying than about preaching!

5. The church is active in evangelism and continually gathers new people to Christ and the church. Members begin new Bible studies and repeat the process of starting new congregations.

6. Mercy is shown to the poor, first to believers who are poor and then also to people who are not yet believers.

7. Members of the church shine as lights of the kingdom of God. They give glory to God by opposing evil and promoting what is good. They defend the truth and promote justice even at the cost of sacrifice and persecution.

STEP 6. PROVIDE FOR THE LIFE AND GROWTH OF THE CHURCH

It is not enough to gather new believers and organize churches. Christ wants churches to grow in faith, love, and service, as well as in number. Leaders must give careful attention to the following:

1. Worship

Jesus said that his heavenly Father wants to be worshipped, and worshipped "in spirit and in truth" (John 4:23). This means that our worship must come from our hearts and be in accordance with the Word of truth, the Bible.

The elements of Christian worship are the following:

- singing of psalms, hymns, and spiritual songs;
- praying, both together and individually;
- reading from the Bible;
- preaching and receiving instruction from the Word of God;
- giving tithes and offerings;
- expressing unity of faith (some churches recite the Apostles' Creed in unison);
- giving and receiving the blessing of God.

2. The Holy Communion

Celebrate Holy Communion at least four times a year to strengthen the faith of the members. First Corinthians

11:23–34 gives instruction about how Holy Communion should be observed.

3. Holiness

Encourage the members to live holy lives by means of the preaching and teaching of the Word of God, prayer, and warnings about sin and "the devil's schemes" (Ephesians 6:11).

4. Discipline

If members fall into sin, show them their error from the Scriptures, pray with them, and urge them to repent and follow Christ in righteousness and truth. If they refuse, remove them so that the name of Christ will not be dishonored, or other members may be tempted to abandon the faith and disobey God.

5. Education

Teach the children, youth, and adults the Word of God through classes, literature, videos, and any means that will build their faith and understanding. Encourage them to share with others what they have learned.

6. Offerings

Encourage members to be generous toward the poor. Gather offerings weekly to support pastors and evangelists who give up ordinary means of supporting themselves in order to serve the Lord. Offerings are expressions of gratitude to God for his mercy to us.

7. Evangelism

Invite people who are not yet believers to attend the services of worship and to hear the gospel. Work for the growth of the churches through the conversion of more and more new people. Multiply the number of Bible studies in various places and help them to grow until they become churches.

8. Leaders

Train the different types of leaders by following the example of the apostles in the New Testament.

a. Leaders who work principally among the members of the church explaining the Bible, visiting homes, praying for the sick, teaching children and youth, and caring for the spiritual well-being of the members are called *elders* in the Bible (Acts 14:23; 1 Timothy 3:1–7; 5:17–20; Titus 1:5–9).

b. Certain elders may be chosen to be called *pastors* because they demonstrate the spiritual gifts required to lead and strengthen the church (Acts 20:28; Ephesians 4:11–12).

c. *Deacons* are leaders who serve the church in a variety of ways, especially by receiving the offerings and serving the poor. The spiritual and moral qualities expected of deacons as well as elders are taught in 1 Timothy 3:1–13.

d. Churches need *evangelists* to provide leadership in announcing the gospel to those who are not yet believers (Ephesians 4:11). Evangelists who are sent to people in distant places are often called *missionaries,* which means "people who are sent."

Make the training of local leaders a high priority.

a. Study Acts 20:17–38, the story of how the apostle Paul established the church at Ephesus. Training local leaders was a priority for the apostle Paul. It must be a high priority for all who desire to multiply churches.

b. Recognize that for churches to be strong and healthy, they need leaders who are called by God, gifted by the Holy Spirit, respected in the community for their moral living, and committed to serving the Lord and his church.

c. Training leaders is a process. At the beginning of the

process only the evangelists know what is true and right and what has to be done. At this stage they must make all the decisions and do and teach everything.

Gradually things change as certain members accept responsibility and learn to carry out the different ministries of the church well.

The process is completed when a group of local people knows what is true, what is right, and what has to be done, *and they are committed to serving the Lord and his church.*

How long to stay and when to leave

a. Nobody can predict precisely how much time the process will require. Pray that local leaders who are competent (*they know what the church needs from them*) and committed (*they are willing to serve faithfully and sacrificially*) will soon appear. Churches remain dependent and immature and fall easily into serious trouble without competent and committed local leaders. Church planters need to stay until local leaders are in place.

b. Remember that when local leaders are ready to take responsibility, *you must move out of the way and let them lead!* Avoid the mistake of trying to remain in control. Instead, like the apostle Paul, place them in the hands of God and move on.

9. Relations Between Churches

Try to establish relations with other churches that teach and worship as you do. Churches need one another for mutual encouragement and assistance, and sometimes for correction. Isolation can be as harmful for churches as it is for individuals.

10. Buildings

A private home may serve well when members are few. You will need a larger place as the number of members increases. Try to get a place that is adequate for worship services, instruction, and fellowship. A building is not the church, but an adequate building is important for the church to carry out its ministries.

11. Prayer

Make every church you start a fellowship of prayer and intercession. Make the Bible study groups centers of prayer. Pray for the leaders and pray for the members. Pray for the strong and the weak. Pray for evangelists and missionaries who preach the gospel in other places. Pray for every teacher who tells children about Christ.

Remember that God does things in answer to prayer that would not happen if the people of God did not pray. Therefore, preach the gospel with passion. Make every church that you begin, in the words of Jesus, a "house of prayer" (Matthew 21:13).

Bibliography

Allen, Roland. *Missionary Methods: St. Paul's or Ours.* London: World Dominion, 1953.

————. *The Spontaneous Expansion of the Church: And the Causes Which Hinder It.* London: World Dominion, 1956.

Bavinck, Johan Herman. *The Impact of Christianity on the Non-Christian World.* Grand Rapids: Eerdmans, 1949.

Bavinck, Johan Herman. *An Introduction to the Science of Missions.* Translated by David Hugh Freeman. Grand Rapids: Baker, 1960.

Boer, Harry R. *Pentecost and Missions.* Grand Rapids: Eerdmans, 1961.

Bosch, David. *Transforming Missions: Paradigm Shifts in Theology of Mission.* Maryknoll, N.Y.: Orbis, 1991.

Blauw, Johannes. *The Missionary Nature of the Church: A Survey of the Biblical Theology of Mission.* New York: McGraw-Hill, 1962.

DuBose, Francis M. *God Who Sends: A Fresh Quest for Biblical Mission.* Nashville, Tenn.: Broadman, 1983.

Goodell, Charles L. *Pastor and Evangelist.* New York: George H. Doran, 1922.

Green, Michael. *Evangelism in the Early Church.* London: Hodder and Stoughton, 1970.

Hedlund, Roger E. *The Mission of the Church in the World: A Biblical Theology.* Grand Rapids: Baker, 1991.

Hendriksen, William. *New Testament Commentary: Exposition of the Pastoral Epistles.* Grand Rapids: Baker, 1957.

Hiebert, Paul G. *Anthropological Insights for Missionaries.* Grand Rapids: Baker, 1985.

Larkin, William J., Jr., and Joel F. Williams. *Mission in the New Testament: An Evangelical Approach.* Maryknoll, N.Y.: Orbis, 1998.

Laubach, Frank. *You Are My Friends.* New York: Harper and Brothers, 1944.

Miller, John. "Prayer and Evangelism." *The Pastor-Evangelist.* Edited by Roger S. Greenway. Phillipsburg, N.J.: Presbyterian and Reformed, 1987.

Mott, John R. *The Pastor and Modern Missions: A Plea for Leadership in World Evangelization.* New York: Student Volunteer Movement for Foreign Missions, 1904.

Murray, Andrew. *Key to the Missionary Problem.* Contemporized by Leona F. Choy. Fort Washington, Pa.: Christian Literature Crusade, 1979.

Pierson, Arthur T. *The Divine Enterprise of Missions: A Series of Lectures Delivered at New Brunswick, NJ.* New York: Baker and Taylor, 1891.

Reformed Ecumenical Synod (R.E.C.). *The Unique Person and Work of Christ.* Grand Rapids, Mich., 1996.

Singhal, Mahendra. "The Cost of Conversion." *World Evangelization* 15/53, 1988.

Speer, Robert E. *The Finality of Jesus Christ.* New York: Fleming H. Revell, 1933.

Verkuyl, Johannes. *Contemporary Missiology.* Translated and edited by Dale Cooper. Grand Rapids: Eerdmans, 1978.

Zwemer, Samuel M. *Thinking Missions with Christ.* Grand Rapids: Zondervan, 1935.